Inflation and Unemployment

Inflation and Unemployment

Macroeconomics with a Range of Equilibria

Ian M. McDonald

University of Melbourne

Basil Blackwell

British Library Cataloguing in Publication Data

A CIP catalogue record for this book is available from the British Library.

Library of Congress Cataloging in Publication Data

McDonald, Ian Martin.
   Inflation and unemployment; macroeconomics with a range of
equilibria/Ian M. McDonald.
      p.   cm.
   Includes bibliographical references.
   ISBN 0-631-17301-3
      1. Unemployment—Effect of inflation on—Mathematical models.
   2. Macroeconomics—Mathematical models.   3. Equilibrium (Economics)
   —Mathematical models.   I. Title.
   HD5710. M34   1989
   339—dc20   89-29614
                                                                      CIP

Typeset in 11 on 13 pt Sabon
by Graphicraft Typesetters Ltd., Hong Kong.
Printed in Great Britain by T.J. Press Ltd., Padstow, Cornwall

Contents

To Daina

Preface

The ideas in this book have been developed over a number of years. In that process a number of people have helped. Early on I had the good fortune to collaborate with Robert Solow. Working with him was an education – it was also a lot of fun. The theory that we developed of bargaining between a group of workers and an employer is a fundamental ingredient in the analysis in this book. Solow also encouraged my interest in the analysis of customer markets, another fundamental ingredient in the theory of a range of equilibria. Karen Spindler gave excellent research assistance for the empirical investigations into customer-market analysis, which form the basis of chapter 4. David Vines and John Creedy gave detailed comments on the initial manuscript, and these led to substantial reorganization and changes. Other colleagues who have helped in various ways over the years include Jim Perkins, Peter Dixon, Jeff Borland, Rob Hocking, Alan Powell, Jocelyn Horne, Charlie Bean, Yew-Kwang Ng, Brian Parmenter, Hugh Sibly, Alistair Watson, Peter Lloyd and Sam Ouliaris. Daina McDonald made a number of editorial suggestions for improving this book and earlier papers on related topics. Margaret Lochran typed the manuscript and its revisions with her usual degree of professional excellence.

I would also like to thank the editors of *Applied Economics* for permission to include here work published in their journal.

Part 1
Introduction

1 The Problem of Stagflation

The relation between inflation and unemployment observed in most industrialized countries is hard to reconcile with the theory of the natural rate of unemployment. According to the natural rate theory, a rate of unemployment which is greater than the natural rate of unemployment will lead to a declining rate of inflation. However, the historical record shows that high levels of unemployment have not led to a declining rate of inflation. Consider the study by Phillips (1958) of wage inflation and unemployment. The seven trade cycles in the United Kingdom between 1861 and 1913 reveal no tendency for a high level of unemployment to generate a *declining* rate of inflation. Instead, for that data set, the rate of wage inflation stuck at around zero when unemployment was high. A similar constancy of the rate of wage inflation was observed by Phillips for the 16-year period of high unemployment from 1923 to 1939 (see Phillips, 1958, figure 9).

Unemployment rates in many industrialized countries have been considered to be at excessive levels since the first oil price shock of 1973. According to the theory of the natural rate of unemployment, a decade and a half of excess supply in the labour market should have led to a declining level of wages and prices. With a level of unemployment greater than the natural rate there is an excess supply of labour. Following the natural rate theory, the excess supply of labour should unleash disequilibrium forces which, sooner or later, should cause the levels of wages and prices to fall.

However, in most industrialized countries the rates of inflation have persisted at positive levels during this long period of high rates of unemployment.

In table 1.1 unemployment rates and inflation rates for six industrialized countries are shown: the unemployment data are also presented in figure 1.1. There is a marked rise in unemployment rates since 1973 in all these countries. To provide a basis for evaluating the natural rate theory, the table and figure also show the average unemployment rate for 1960–4 for each of the countries. In each country, inflation was low in 1964. This suggests, according to the theory of the natural rate of unemployment, that the natural rate was equal to or less than the average unemployment rate for 1960–4. As figure 1.1 shows, rates of unemployment in the 1970s and 1980s were generally well in excess of the 1960–4 average. But this long period of high unemployment did not lead to negative rates of inflation. In 1987, as shown in table 1.1, each of these countries had a positive rate of inflation. Furthermore, although there are differences between countries in the severity of their experience with unemployment, this variation between countries did not lead to the variations in the 1987 inflation rates that would be predicted by the theory of the natural rate of unemployment. Indeed, Australia, which had one of the largest increases in unemployment, ends up with the highest inflation rate. The United States has the smallest increase in unemployment in the 1970s and 1980s compared to the early 1960s and yet at the end of the period had a relatively low inflation rate.

One should consider the possibility that variations in the natural rate of unemployment in these countries have been sufficient to explain the experience in inflation. Figure 1.1, along with table 1.1, can be studied to obtain a rough idea of the complex patterns of the variation in the natural rate of unemployment that would be required in order to generate such an explanation. The size of some of these variations is large. For example, in Australia an approximately threefold increase in the natural rate of unemployment appears to be required to explain the persistently high inflation rate. However, attempts to explain these sorts of movements in the natural rate of unemployment have not been successful. The

Table 1.1 *Unemployment and inflation in six industrialized countries*

	Average unemployment rate, 1960–4	CPI per cent change, 1964	Unemployment rate																CPI per cent change, 1987
			1972	1973	1974	1975	1976	1977	1978	1979	1980	1981	1982	1983	1984	1985	1986	1987	
Australia	2.1	2.3	2.6	2.3	2.7	4.9	4.7	5.6	6.3	6.2	6.0	5.7	7.1	9.9	8.9	8.2	8.0	8.1	8.5
Canada	5.6	1.9	6.2	5.5	5.3	6.9	7.1	8.1	8.3	7.4	7.5	7.5	11.1	11.9	11.3	10.5	9.6	8.9	4.4
France	1.2	3.0	2.8	2.7	3.0	4.3	4.5	5.0	5.4	6.0	6.4	7.6	8.2	8.4	9.9	10.2	10.5	10.6	3.1
Germany	0.7	2.3	0.9	1.0	2.1	4.0	3.9	3.7	3.3	3.3	3.3	4.6	6.7	8.2	8.2	8.3	8.0	7.9	0.2
UK	1.5	3.4	3.1	2.1	2.2	3.6	4.8	5.2	5.1	4.5	6.1	9.1	10.4	11.3	11.5	11.7	11.8	10.4	4.2
USA	5.6	1.1	5.6	4.9	5.6	8.3	7.7	7.0	6.1	5.8	7.2	7.6	9.7	9.6	7.5	7.1	7.0	6.2	3.7

Sources: OECD, 1988: *Economic Outlook*, June.
Norton, W. E. and Kennedy, P. J., 1986: *Australia Economic Statistics 1949/50 to 1984/85: 1 Tables*. Reserve Bank of Australia.

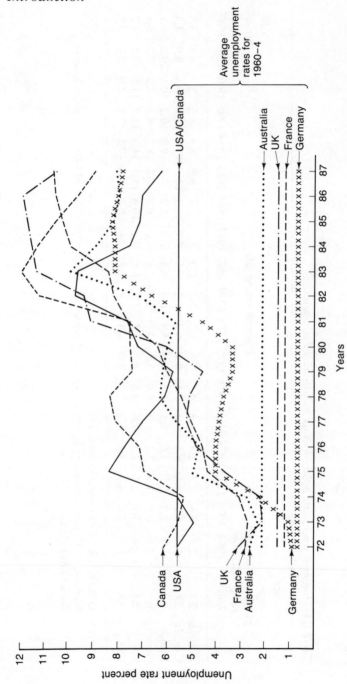

Figure 1.1　Unemployment in six industrialized countries.

survey of the empirical evidence by Johnson and Layard (1986) finds that changes in the composition of the labour force, structural shifts, changes in the replacement ratio, changes in union density and changes in minimum wages can only explain minor changes in the natural rate of unemployment. Allowing for variations in the natural rate of unemployment fails to reconcile the theory of the natural rate with the observed behaviour of inflation and unemployment.

The data in table 1.1 suggest 16 years of excess supply of labour. A simple measure of the total excess supply over this period is the cumulative excess unemployment rate; that is, the sum of the annual excess of the unemployment rate over the average unemployment rate of 1960–4. As an example, for Australia this calculation gives a figure of 63.6. For comparative purposes it is better to express the cumulative excess unemployment rate as an average for the years of cumulation. For Australia this average is 3.98 (=63.6/16). In figure 1.2 is plotted, for each of the six countries, the average of the cumulative excess unemployment rate for the period 1972–87 on the horizontal axis and the percent changes in the CPI in 1987 on the vertical axis. One can see from figure 1.2 that there is no suggestion of the negative relation that would be implied by the standard theory of demand and supply. Furthermore, figure 1.2 reinforces the view that these countries have suffered from considerable excess supply in the labour market, and yet inflation remains generally positive. For 16 years these countries have averaged 1.5 or more percentage points per annum of unemployment in excess of the early 1960s average. For Australia, the UK, France and Germany the average annual excess of unemployment over the early 1960s average was more than four percentage points. But inflation remained positive.

The degree of excess supply in the labour market is probably greater than is revealed by the official unemployment statistics. It is widely held that the discouraged-worker effect has led to large numbers of 'hidden' unemployed in these countries in this period. According to the theory of the natural rate, the hidden unemployed should have exerted downward pressure on inflation. Their failure to do this casts further doubt on the theory of the natural rate of unemployment.

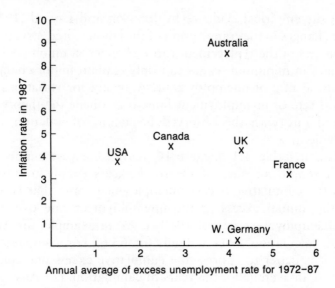

Figure 1.2   Inflation and 16 years of excess unemployment in six industrialized countries.

While high rates of unemployment do not produce declining rates of inflation, the experience of industrialized economies shows that low rates of unemployment are associated with increasing rates of inflation. This pattern is not that suggested by the theory of the natural rate of unemployment. According to the natural rate theory, the downward pressure on the rate of inflation caused by high levels of unemployment should be of a strength comparable to the upward pressure on inflation caused by rates of unemployment below the natural rate. That this symmetrical behaviour is not observed is further evidence against the theory of the natural rate of unemployment.

It is the presumption of this book that macroeconomic models in which there is a *range* of equilibrium levels of unemployment offer a more fruitful basis for the explanation of the relation between inflation and unemployment than do models in which there is a natural rate of unemployment. The aim of this book is to develop some macroeconomic models which have a range of equilibria, and to discuss the implications for macroeconomic policy of the existence of such an equilibrium range.

1.1 Involuntary Unemployment

The macroeconomic models developed in this book generate involuntary unemployment. The range of equilibria in these models is a range of involuntary unemployment. An unemployed person is defined as involuntarily unemployed if she has not received a job offer and her reservation wage is less than the wage paid to a person of equal skill. By this definition, when workers are laid off, unemployment is imposed on them and they are involuntarily unemployed. It is involuntary unemployment that the models of this book seek to explain.

According to the definition given above of a person who is involuntarily unemployed, the state of unemployment is involuntary in an *ex post* sense. It may be that, *ex ante*, people choose voluntarily an action which entails a risk of unemployment. However, the possibility that unemployment is voluntary in an *ex ante* sense has little practical value. Any state of affairs may be considered voluntary in an *ex ante* sense. In the labour market it is the *ex post* outcomes that are observed.

The explanation of involuntary unemployment is emphasized in this book because of the importance of that type of unemployment in industrialized economies. As discussed by Tobin (1972) there is plenty of evidence of the existence of involuntary unemployment. Furthermore, involuntary unemployment is a serious economic problem because it imposes heavy costs on people. By comparison, the burden of voluntary unemployment is not onerous. A reduction in the extent of involuntary unemployment would be a significant improvement in people's welfare.

1.2 The Outline of the Book

The growing disillusion with the theory of the natural rate of unemployment has led to the development of several alternative approaches to macroeconomics. Some of these are briefly reviewed in chapter 2. Then the basis for the theory of the range of equilibria, the alternative theory favoured in this book, is explained. It is shown how a range of equilibria can be reasonably derived from customer market analysis. Customer market analysis is the common basis of the four macroeconomic models with ranges of equilibrium levels of involuntary unemployment developed in this book.

In chapter 3 the analysis of the determination of retail prices in a customer market is set out, first for a retailer selling one good and then for a retailer selling many types of goods. In chapter 4 empirical evidence on the behaviour of retail prices is reviewed and shown to be consistent with customer market analysis.

The macroeconomic models developed in this book seek to explain involuntary unemployment. Broadly speaking, explanations about the causes of involuntary unemployment (that is, the causes of wages exceeding the reservation wages of workers) can be classified into two groups. The first is the theory of efficiency wages. This theory, which has at its core the assumption that individuals try to maximize their utility, argues that wages exceed reservation wages in order to promote the efficiency of the production process. Yellen (1984) explains how high wages can reduce shirking, reduce turnover, improve the quality of job applicants and raise morale. In the model of chapter 5, goods are sold in customer markets and high wages improve the efficiency of the production process. The model is shown to generate a range of equilibrium levels of involuntary unemployment.

A second explanation of the cause of involuntary unemployment is the setting of wages to maximize the utility of a group. By forcing unemployment on some individuals the group may gain. Models based on this idea are developed in chapters 6, 7 and 8. In chapter 6 it is shown that the sharing between a group of workers and an employer of rents arising from specific human capital can lead to involuntary unemployment of some members of the group. It is argued that the group is able to impose its wishes by various types of informal pressure and to prevent the undercutting of wages by unemployed individuals. In addition, the group may form itself into a trade union to facilitate the pursuit of its interest. However, a trade union, being a more powerful body, may attempt to appropriate other rents, such as those arising from the market power of firms in selling their goods. In chapters 7 and 8 these actions are shown to be another source of involuntary unemployment and, when combined with customer market analysis, to yield ranges of equilibrium levels of involuntary unemployment.

When wages are determined by the maximization of the utility of a group, the group may gain at the expense of individuals who are forced into unemployment. This mechanism can generate involuntary unemployment, whether or not the interests of the unemployed individuals appear in the group's collective utility function. In chapter 7 the trade union is assumed to have an 'open-door' policy with regard to members, accepting new members and according them full weight in its utility function. In chapter 8 the trade union is assumed to be dominated by a group of insiders who enjoy secure employment. Both the open and the insider-dominated trade union are shown to be capable of generating involuntary unemployment.

While the contrast between behaviour aimed at maximizing an individual's utility (which underlies the theory of efficiency wages) and behaviour aimed at maximizing the collective utility of a group is a useful one, it can be carried too far. After all, it is individuals who choose to form or join groups. In the models developed in this book the maximization of the expected utility of each member of a group generates a similar wage demand to that generated by the maximization of the collective welfare of the group. This point should be borne in mind when reading about the models in chapters 6, 7 and 8.

The models developed in this book provide a basis for an explanation of stagflation. Moving from explanation to the formulation of economic policy, the analysis in chapter 9 suggests that an active policy of aggregate demand management will generate a tendency for the rate of inflation to increase. For an economy with a range of equilibrium levels of unemployment, it appears to be impossible to discover the minimum equilibrium level of unemployment without overshooting this rate of unemployment and causing inflation to increase. If there were a natural rate of unemployment, the consequences of such an overshooting would be reversible at relatively small cost. But with a range of equilibrium levels of unemployment, aggregate demand is an expensive policy for reducing inflation. Using the theory of the range of equilibria, some alternative anti-inflationary policies are discussed in chapter 9.

2 *Alternative Views*

Models of the natural rate of unemployment yield a vertical long-run Phillips curve, as shown in figure 2.1. A government policy aimed at keeping the level of unemployment below the equilibrium, or 'natural', rate (shown as U_1 in figure 2.1) by maintaining a high level of aggregate demand will lead to an increasing rate of inflation. On the other hand, a government policy of setting aggregate demand sufficiently low to induce a level of unemployment in excess of U_1, the equilibrium rate, should, according to the models, lead to a decreasing rate of inflation. It is this latter prediction which was argued in chapter 1 to be inconsistent with the behaviour of inflation and unemployment observed in industrialized economies.

The theory of the natural rate of unemployment has been extended by introducing processes which generate an effect of hysteresis (see especially Hargreaves–Heap, 1980; Mitchell, 1987; Blanchard and Summers, 1986). According to hysteresis, the equilibrium level of unemployment adjusts towards the actual level of unemployment. As a result of this adjustment an aggregate demand policy which raises the actual level of unemployment will also cause the equilibrium level of unemployment to rise. Once the equilibrium level has caught up with the actual level, the disequilibrium pressures of excess supply on prices and wages disappear and inflation ceases to decrease.

Hargreaves–Heap (1980) and Mitchell (1987) emphasize the

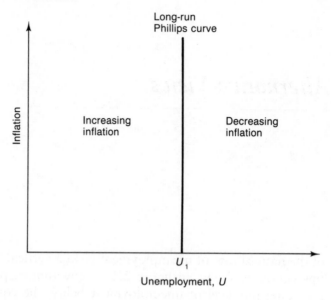

Figure 2.1

deskilling of the unemployed as the microfoundation for the hys-teresial effect. Those laid off lose their job skills while unem-ployed. Having lost their job skills they cease to compete with the employed for jobs and so cease to exert downward pressure on wages.

The idea of deskilling does not offer a persuasive reason for the persistence of inflation at high levels of unemployment. It is implausible that skills are lost quickly and easily by workers when they are unemployed. If skills are so ephemeral, an explanation of why workers do not make greater efforts to avoid being laid off would be required to yield a convincing theory. And even if the apparent short-sightedness of employees facing lay-off could be explained, the theory would also have to explain why the deskilled unemployed refuse unskilled jobs.

Blanchard and Summers (1986) have put forward an alternative basis for a hysteresial effect. They argue that union wage-setting is dominated by the employed. Under certain circumstances this dominance causes employment to contract. Even at high rates of unemployment, the unemployed, having no influence on wage

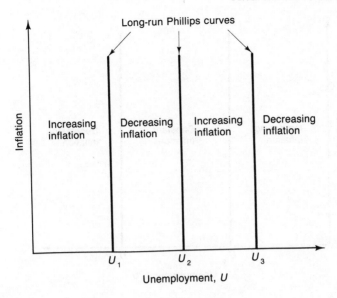

Figure 2.2

demands, do not cause the rate of inflation to fall. These ideas have also been developed in a series of papers by Lindbeck and Snower (1984, 1985, 1988a,b). They use the nomenclature 'insider' and 'outsider' to denote employed workers and unemployed workers. In chapter 8 of this book, the insider – outsider distinction is explored in the analysis of the wage demands of an insider-dominated trade union. That analysis casts doubt on the ability of these theories to generate hysteresis.

Theories of multiple equilibria have been put forward by Diamond (1981, 1982) and Howitt (1985). These theories emphasize the role of externalities in job search. The authors have emphasized the possibility that arises from these theories of the existence of two or more equilibrium unemployment rates. If multiple equilibria exist it is possible that the economy could jump from one equilibrium to another. For example, in figure 2.2 three long-run Phillips curves corresponding to three equilibrium levels of unemployment are shown. The middle level, U_2, corresponds to an unstable equilibrium, while U_1 and U_3 are stable equilibria. The relation between direction of change of inflation and the level

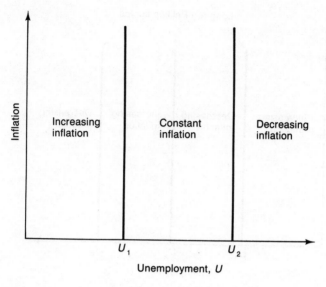

Figure 2.3

of unemployment is peculiar. A region of increasing inflation separates two regions of decreasing inflation. Therefore, if unemployment is between U_1 and U_2 in figure 2.2 then inflation is decreasing. But higher levels of unemployment, between U_2 and U_3, lead to increasing inflation. This pattern of inflation and unemployment is not observed in industrialized economies. This suggests that these theories of multiple equilibria offer implausible explanations of stagflation.

A number of models that yield a range of equilibrium levels of employment are developed in this book. The relation between inflation and unemployment predicted by such models is illustrated in figure 2.3. U_1 is the level of unemployment that corresponds with the highest equilibrium level of employment, while U_2 corresponds to the lowest equilibrium level of employment. For levels of unemployment between U_1 and U_2 there are no disequilibrium forces causing the rate of inflation to change. As a consequence, for any level of unemployment between U_1 and U_2, inflation will tend to remain constant. Only outside the equilibrium range, that is only for levels of unemployment less than U_1 or greater than U_2, will the disequilibrium forces cause the rate of inflation to change.

2.1   Imperfect Competition and a Unique Equilibrium

The standard theory of imperfect competition does not provide a reasonable basis for a range of equilibrium levels of employment. Consider an economy with z firms. Each firm faces a downward-sloping demand curve. An example, labelled q_1^d for one of the z firms, is shown in figure 2.4. A decrease in the level of aggregate demand will shift the firm's demand curve to the left. In figure 2.4 the demand curve q_2^d corresponds to a lower level of aggregate demand. For this particular firm, the lower level of aggregate demand would lead to sales of q_2 at a price of p_1. The price is measured in monetary units. In figure 2.5 the curve labelled m_1 is the marginal revenue product of labour schedule arising from the demand curve q_1^d. The level of employment, n_1, which is the profit-maximizing level if the money wage is w_1, is assumed to produce a level of output of q_1.

To generate a macroeconomic equilibrium, assume that the z firms are identical and that zn_1 units of labour are supplied at a real wage of w_1/p_1. Then $\{p_1, q_1, w_1, n_1\}$ is a macroequilibrium. Under what circumstances could there exist another macroequilibrium?

Consider a decrease in the level of aggregate demand which shifts the demand curve facing each of the z firms to q_2^d. Assume that the elasticity of the demand curve at the price p_1 is unaffected by the shift of the demand curve. (This assumption of an isoelastic shift is relaxed later.) The marginal revenue product of labour curve also shifts to the left. In figure 2.5 three possibilities are shown. The curve m_2' represents decreasing returns to labour, m_2'' represents constant returns to labour and m_2''' represents increasing returns to labour. In the case of diminishing returns to labour, q_2 is produced by the level of employment n_2'. For constant returns to labour, q_2 is produced by n_2'', and for increasing returns to labour q_2 is produced by n_2'''.

For the case of constant returns to labour, a macroeconomic

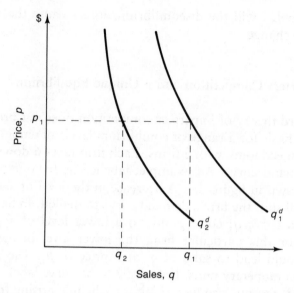

Figure 2.4

equilibrium can exist with the lower level of demand represented by the product demand curve q_2^d if zn_2'' units of labour are supplied at a real wage of w_1/p_1. This would require the labour supply curve to be horizontal. With constant returns to labour, the requirement of a horizontal labour supply curve is not merely sufficient but also necessary for multiple equilibria. To see the necessity, consider an upward-sloping labour supply curve, going through w_1/p_1, zn_1, requiring a real wage of w_4/p_1 to induce an aggregate labour supply of zn_2'', where $w_4 < w_1$. In figure 2.5 the point $\{w_4, n_2''\}$ lies below m_2'', inducing unemployed labour to bid the money wage down and causing employment to increase above n_2''. Each firm would then produce more than q_2, forcing the price of output down. The decline in the price of output would increase the downward pressure on the money wage exerted by people wishing to work. Both wages and prices would fall. The argument works in reverse for increases in demand. That is, rightward shifts in the demand curve from q_1^d will cause wages and prices to increase.

While figures 2.4 and 2.5 are helpful in order to understand how a decline in demand will lead to falling wages and prices, it

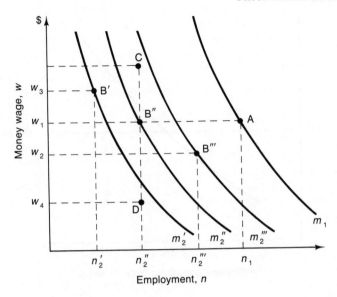

Figure 2.5

is easier to see that there is a unique macroequilibrium level by examining the aggregate labour market depicted in figure 2.6. For profits to be maximized at each of the z identical firms, the money wage has to equal the marginal revenue product of labour. Marginal revenue equals $p(1 - 1/\eta)$, where η is the elasticity of demand for the firm's output. With all firms in the economy maximizing profits, the following equation will hold:

$$w/p = (1 - 1/\eta)M$$

where M, called the aggregate marginal product of labour, is the common value of the firms' marginal products of labour. With constant returns to labour at each firm, M is independent of the aggregate level of employment, N. Assuming that η is constant, the schedule of $(1 - 1/\eta)M$ is also independent of N, and is shown in figure 2.6 as a horizontal line. The upward-sloping aggregate supply of labour schedule, L^s, cuts $M(1 - 1/\eta)$ once, determining the unique equilibrium level of employment. Thus, if there are constant returns to labour and if the labour supply curve is not horizontal, there can only be one macroeconomic equilibrium.

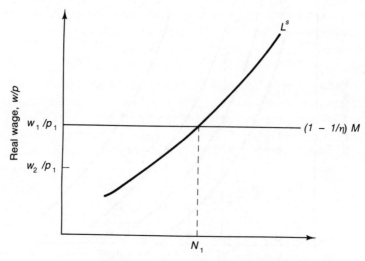

Figure 2.6

Returning to figure 2.5, with increasing returns to labour the marginal product of the n_2'' unit of labour is less than the marginal product of the n_1 unit of labour. In consequence, the marginal revenue product of labour at n_2''' is less than w_1. For there to be a macroequilibrium with a level of employment of zn_2''', the aggregate labour supply curve would have to be upward sloping by a degree just sufficient to induce a labour supply of zn_2''' at a real wage of w_2/p_1. A labour supply curve of greater or lesser slope would not yield a macroequilibrium with employment at the level zn_2'''. In terms of the aggregate picture in figure 2.6, with increasing returns to labour the curve of $(1 - 1/\eta)M$ would slope upwards. For there to be a second macroequilibrium at a real wage equal to w_2/p_1 the aggregate supply of labour schedule would have to be such as to slope upwards so as to cut $(1 - 1/\eta)M$ exactly at w_2/p_1.

With diminishing returns to labour, the marginal revenue product of labour at n_2' exceeds w_1. For there to be a macroeconomic equilibrium, the labour supply curve would have to slope downwards and induce a labour a supply of zn_2' units of labour at a real wage of w_3/p_1.

The preceding analysis shows that a range of equilibria is unlikely to arise from the standard model of imperfect competition. The condition for a range of equilibria is that the elasticity of the aggregate labour supply schedule has to equal the elasticity of employment with respect to the marginal product of labour. Since these elasticities are derived from different foundations (from the preferences of individuals on one hand, and from the technology of production on the other hand) their equality would be a coincidence. In practice, the elasticity of the aggregate labour supply schedule appears to be a small positive number, while the elasticity of employment with respect to the real value of the marginal revenue product of labour, that is with respect to $(1 - 1/\varepsilon)M$, is -4 or less. (With a Cobb–Douglas production function, this elasticity is $1/(\beta - 1)$, where β, the elasticity of output with respect to employment, is 0.75 or more.)

Relaxing the assumption that the elasticity of product demand is unaffected by shifts in demand does not increase the likelihood of a range of equilibria. Suppose, for example, that the elasticity of demand increases in booms. Rotemberg and Saloner (1986) have put forward an argument for this phenomenon. In their model, producers, on cutting price, enjoy a larger increase in sales when the market is larger. A larger market arises in boom conditions. A higher elasticity of demand in a boom will, with constant returns to labour, raise the marginal revenue product of labour in a boom. For multiple equilibria a point such as C in figure 2.5 would have to be consistent with the aggregate supply of labour. The aggregate supply of labour curve would have to slope upwards, by exactly the right amount.

2.2 Customer Markets and a Range of Equilibria

For many items, purchasers do not search among potential suppliers before each purchase. Instead, purchasers frequent or patronize a particular seller and search relatively infrequently. Consumers shop at the same supermarket week after week, and only occasionally sample the prices offered by competing supermarkets. Search is particularly infrequent relative to the frequency of purchase for low-value items such as food, pharmaceuticals etc.

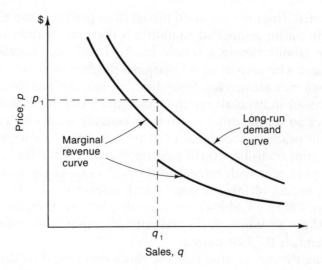

Figure 2.7

Even for high-value items the consumer will tend to begin search at a supplier previously known to him or her.

A low frequency of search relative to the frequency of purchase is the crucial characteristic of a customer market. As will be shown in chapter 3, this characteristic of search behaviour implies a vertical discontinuity in the marginal revenue curve at the actual level of sales. An example is depicted in figure 2.7, where q_1 is the actual level of sales at a price of p_1.

A vertical discontinuity in the marginal revenue curve can yield a range of macroeconomic equilibria. To see this, consider figures 2.8 and 2.9. In figure 2.8, two demand curves facing a representative firm are drawn, reflecting two levels of aggregate demand. Assuming that this firm sells in a customer market, the two 'stepped' marginal revenue product of labour curves are drawn in figure 2.9. The steps occur at the levels of employment, n_1 and n_2, required to produce output levels of q_1 and q_2 respectively. Assuming diminishing returns to labour, the top of the step at the employment level of n_1 is lower than the top of the step at n_2. As long as the labour supply curve is not too steep there can be macroequilibria at n_1 and at n_2. For example, if zn_1 units of labour

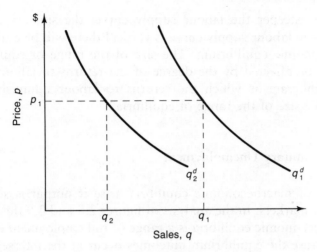

Figure 2.8

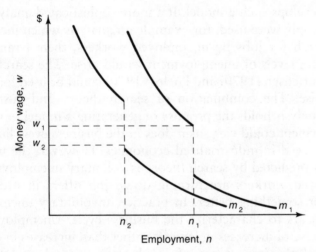

Figure 2.9

are supplied at a real wage of w_1/p_1 and zn_2 units of labour are supplied at a real wage of w_2/p_1, then both n_1 and n_2 can be macroequilibria. Furthermore, if n_1 and n_2 are macroequilibria then there will be macroequilibria at all the employment levels in between n_1 and n_2. A range of macroeconomic equilibria will exist. The steeper the labour supply curve, the smaller is this range. If the labour supply curve is vertical there will be a unique macroeconomic equilibrium. The size of the range of equilibria will also be affected by the degree of the returns to labour: the smaller the rate at which the returns to labour diminish, the greater the size of the range of equilibria.

2.3   Involuntary Unemployment

A range of macroeconomic equilibria arise if output is sold in customer markets. In the analysis of figures 2.8 and 2.9 the range of macroeconomic equilibria is a range of full employment equilibria because the equilibrium outcomes occur at the intersections of the labour supply and labour demand schedules. Woglom (1982) develops such a model. If a more sophisticated analysis of labour supply were used, for example an analysis which incorporated search for jobs by unemployed workers, then a range of equilibrium levels of unemployment would arise. The search theory of Mortensen (1970) and Phelps (1970) could be used for such an exercise. The combination of search theory and customer market analysis holds the promise of generating a model in which unemployment could vary, as it does in the business cycle fluctuations observed in industrialized economies. However, the unemployment predicted by search theory is voluntary unemployment. Unemployed workers are turning down job offers in order to search for something better. In practice, involuntary unemployment appears to characterize the business cycle. Unemployment rises because of increases in lay-offs rather than increases in quits. Because of the importance of involuntary unemployment, the search theory of voluntary unemployment is eschewed in the macroeconomic models developed in this book.

Part 2
Customer Markets

3   Retailing in a Customer Market

In the standard economic theory of the firm, the response of sales to changes in price is assumed to occur instantaneously. Of course, it is widely recognized that in practice the response of sales to changes in price is gradual rather than instantaneous; see, for example, Phelps and Winters (1970) for a model which allows for a gradual response of sales to price changes. Customer market analysis suggests not only that sales response is gradual, but also that for a significant group of products the response of sales to a price decrease is *slower* than the response of sales to a price increase.

This differential response rate occurs for those products for which it is not efficient for buyers to search among sellers before each purchase. Low-value items, such as food and pharmaceuticals, tend to have this characteristic. Search may occur now and again, but the crucial characteristic is that the frequency of searching is less than the frequency of purchasing. Having decided on the best seller from whom to buy, buyers will patronize that seller, purchasing the good repeatedly. Changes in the prices of goods offered by a seller will quickly become apparent to that seller's own clientele. However, to broadcast a price change to those buyers who purchase from other sellers is more difficult. To rely on the unassisted spread of information takes time: to advertise costs money. The implication of this structure of information flows is that a seller will perceive an asymmetry in the responsiveness of sales to price increases compared with the responsiveness of sales to price decreases. A price increase will lead to a rapid loss in sales as customers learn quickly of the new price and turn to other sellers. A price decrease will increase sales at a similarly rapid rate only if the seller incurs the cost of advertising. Without advertising, price decreases lead to only a gradual rise in sales.

A rough idea of the size of the customer market sector can be derived by adding up the sales of those categories of goods bought by consumers in customer markets. If customer markets are thought to be restricted to low-value items then these customer market categories may be thought of as follows (bracketed figures show the percentages of total consumer expenditure accounted for by the category, as given in Jackson, 1982, p. 106, table 3.3): food (17.2); alcoholic drink (7.5); tobacco (3.6); clothing (7.3); books, newspapers and magazines (1.4); chemists' goods (1.6); miscellaneous recreational goods (3.0); other miscellaneous goods (1.9); running costs of motor vehicles (6.3); entertainment and recreational services (2.0); catering (meals and accommodation) (5.5); domestic service (0.5); other household goods (that is, other than durables) (2.7). These categories accounted for 60.5 per cent of total consumer expenditure and 36.3 per cent of gross domestic product. However, the basic asymmetry in the response of sales to cuts in price compared with the response to increases in price may extend to high-value items. For an individual engaged in search, Stiglitz has drawn attention to '. . . the asymmetry of information that is created . . . the moment an individual arrives at a store. He knows the price at that store; he knows only the distribution of prices at other stores' (Stiglitz, 1987, p. 1043).

3.1   Dynamics of the Determination of the Number of Customers

Assume that each purchaser checks the prices of goods offered by each potential supplier once every T periods. In keeping with the above description of a customer market, the number of periods between each purchase of the good, or the basket of goods, is less than T. The determination of T is not modelled here. It suffices to say that purchasers have a strong enough desire to update their knowledge of market prices every T periods. In a more complete model this assumption could be justified by the introduction of forces which lead to the desire by purchasers for periodic search. For example, if customers suspect that there are random productivity shocks to the production technology of alternative shops, which will cause suppliers to change prices, then they may be induced to check out the prices charged by the alternative shops. Sibly (1989) presents a model in which T is determined along these lines.

In this chapter it is assumed that the moment of search is distributed evenly across the population, so that in each time period an equal number of potential purchasers check the prices charged by a particular shop, and that over T periods any shop has had its prices reviewed by all its potential purchasers.

With periodic search by purchasers, a shop that lowers its prices will experience a gradual increase in its clientele as additional purchasers review that shop's price in their periodic search. After T time periods the increase in clientele will come to an end at a level given by the function $c(p)$, with $c'(p) < 0$, where p is the price charged by the shop for the good. It could be assumed that the firm can reduce the length of the customer market build-up period by advertising the cut in price. However, the inclusion of advertising would not overturn the implications of the model for retail-price stickiness. Advertising costs would themselves be asymmetric, since it does not pay to advertise an increase in price. For simplicity advertising costs are ignored.

Alternatively, if a shop raises its price, intensive search is considered by all its customers the next time they visit to make a purchase. How many customers actually decide to conduct an intensive search will depend on the level of the new price, customers' beliefs about prices at other shops and the convenience, at this price, of this supplier compared to other potential suppliers. It is assumed that, when the shop raises its price, the shop's clientele will adjust immediately to the number given by the function $c(p)$.

The relation between the size of the shop's clientele and the price charged by the shop can be summarized in the following way. Let $\{c_0, p_0\}$ describe the initial clientele and price. Assume that c_0 is the equilibrium number of customers for the initial situation, i.e. $c_0 = c(p_0)$. Then for $p < p_0$, a price reduction, the gradual increase in the clientele is described by

$$c_t = c_0 + \{c(p) - c_0\}t/T \quad \text{for } 0 \leqslant t \leqslant T,$$

$$c_t = c(p) \qquad\qquad\qquad \text{for } t \geqslant T \qquad\qquad (3.1a)$$

while for $p \geqslant p_0$ any adjustment to the size of the clientele occurs instantly and so

$$c_t = c(p) \qquad \text{for } t \geqslant 0 \qquad\qquad\qquad\qquad (3.1b)$$

The position of the function $c(p)$ is affected by the customers' beliefs about prices charged by other shops. If customers revise upwards their beliefs about prices at other shops, then c will increase at any value of p. In an inflationary situation, a shop will be able to raise its price in line with the beliefs of its customers about prices at other shops without losing any customers. To avoid clutter, a variable representing these beliefs about prices is not explicitly written into $c(p)$.

3.2 Profit-maximizing Behaviour by a Shop Selling a Single Good

To prepare the way for the analysis of the more complicated multi-good shop presented in the next section, assume here that a shop sells only one good. Assume that each customer has the same demand function $h(p)$, with $h'(p) \leqslant 0$, where p is the retail price of the good. The shop sells $h(p)$ goods to each customer, making total sales at time t equal to $c_t h(p)$.

Assume a simple cost structure for the shop, in which the only marginal cost is the cost to the shopkeeper of the good, called the producer's price, p^p. The shop's other costs are fixed at F. the shopkeeper's decision problem is to set a retail price which maximizes the discounted sum of profits. We assume an infinite time horizon to calculate the discounted sum of profits. Profits are discounted at the rate r. Over this infinite horizon, p^p is expected to remain constant. Pricing strategies in which the retail price varies over time, for example strategies in which p is gradually increased or gradually lowered, are not considered. However, more complicated pricing strategies in which price may be varied over time do not eliminate the asymmetry between the ease with which information about price is transmitted to regular customers and the difficulty with which information about price is transmitted to those buyers who shop at other sellers. In consequence, to allow for variable price strategies would not overturn the implications of the model for retail-price stickiness.

Assume the firm begins with $c(p)$ customers. If the firm maintains or raises its price then the number of customers adjusts instantaneously and the discounted sum of profits is simply

$$\Pi = \int_{t=0}^{\infty} \{h(p)c(p)(p - p^p) - F\}e^{-rt}dt$$
$$= \Pi^{+}(p,p^p,r) \qquad \text{for} \quad p \geqslant p_0 \tag{3.2}$$

where p_0 is the initial price. On the other hand, if the firm lowers its price, the customer build-up period, T, has to be allowed for. The discounted sum of profits at time 0 when the retail price is set below p_0 is

$$\Pi = \int_{t=0}^{T} \{[c(p_0) + (c(p) - c(p_0))t/T]h(p)(p - p^p) - F\}e^{-rt}dt$$
$$+ \int_{t=T}^{\infty} \{c(p)h(p)(p - p^p) - F\}e^{-rt}dt$$
$$= \Pi^{-}(p_0,p,p^p,r,T) \qquad \text{for } p < p_0 \tag{3.3}$$

The firm's problem is to choose p so as to maximize either (3.2) or (3.3), whichever is the greater. The first-order condition for maximizing Π with $p \geqslant p_0$ is obtained by differentiating (3.2) with respect to p, giving

$$h'(p)c(p)(p - p^p) + c'(p)h(p)(p - p^p) + h(p)c(p) = 0 \tag{3.4}$$

(3.4) can be rewritten as

$$p\left[\left(1 - \frac{1}{\eta}\right)\frac{1}{\mu} + \frac{1}{\eta}\right]\bigg/\left(\frac{1}{\mu} + \frac{1}{\eta}\right) = p^p \tag{3.5}$$

where $\eta = h'(p)p/h(p)$ is the elasticity of an individual's demand function with respect to price, and $\mu = c'(p)p/c(p)$ is the elasticity of the number of customers buying from a shop with respect to price. Because equation (3.5) is derived from the first-order condition for a maximization problem with an infinite time horizon, the left-hand side is marginal revenue *per period* and the right-hand side is marginal cost *per period*. For a perfectly competitive firm, $\mu = \infty$, because a small price increase will drive all customers away, and for that case equation (3.5) becomes $p = p^p$. For a firm with some market power, $\mu < \infty$, implying that $p > p^p$. It seems reasonable to assume that most shops have some monopoly power, if only for spatial reasons.

The left-hand side of equation (3.5) looks different from the definition of marginal revenue in the standard theory of demand. This is because sales per customer and the number of customers are not usually distinguished from each other. If sales per customer are constant $(h'(p) = 0)$ so that the number of customers is synonymous with total sales, then the left-hand side of (3.5) is $p(1 - 1/\mu)$, the standard definition of marginal revenue.

The first-order condition for maximizing Π with $p < p_0$ is obtained by differentiating (3.7) with respect to p, giving

$$[h'(p)(p - p^p) + h(p)](X + 1) + c'(p)h(p)(p - p^p)/c(p) = 0 \qquad (3.6)$$

where

$$X = \frac{c(p_0)}{c(p)}\left(\int_{t=0}^{T} e^{-rt}dt - T^{-1}\int_{t=0}^{T} t\,e^{-rt}dt\right)\Bigg/\left(\int_{t=T}^{\infty} e^{-rt}dt + T^{-1}\int_{t=0}^{T} t\,e^{-rt}dt\right)$$

$$= \frac{c(p_0)}{c(p)}\frac{rT - 1 + e^{-rT}}{1 - e^{-rt}} > 0 \qquad \text{for } r,t > 0$$

Equation (3.6) can be rewritten as

$$p\left[\left(1 - \frac{1}{\eta}\right)\frac{(1 + X)}{\mu} + \frac{1}{\eta}\right]\Bigg/\left(\frac{1 + X}{\mu} + \frac{1}{\eta}\right) = p^p \qquad (3.7)$$

The left-hand side of (3.7) is the marginal revenue *per unit of the good sold per period*, and the right-hand side is marginal cost *per*

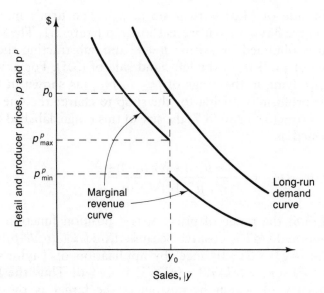

Figure 3.1

unit of the good sold per period. Since sales of the good are not constant in every period following a price cut (but in fact increase during the first T periods) the flows of marginal revenue and marginal cost are expressed in terms of per good sold per period. By contrast, following an increase in price, sales adjust immediately to a level at which they remain constant for the future, and so the 'per good sold' dimension can be suppressed.

The impact of the gradual increase in the number of customers to a price reduction is embodied in the variable X. If $T = 0$ (instantaneous response, as in the case of a price increase) then $X = 0$ and the left-hand side of (3.7) becomes the same as the left-hand side of (3.5). Therefore with $T = 0$ the marginal revenue curve is continuous. If $T > 0$ then $X > 0$. Furthermore, $dX/dT > 0$. $X > 0$ and $\mu < \infty$ imply that the ratio on the left-hand side of (3.7) is less than the ratio on the left-hand side of (3.5). This implies that at the initial level of sales of y_0 and the initial price of p_0, the marginal revenue from a price decrease (the left-hand side of (3.7) with p set at p_0) is less than the marginal revenue from a price increase (the left-hand side of (3.5) with p set at p_0). The firm's marginal revenue curve has a step at y_0, as shown in figure 3.1. The size of this step is obtained by setting $p = p_0$ and substracting the left-hand side of (3.7) from the left-hand side of (3.5). For any producer price lying in the range of p^p_{min} to p^p_{max} (as shown in figure 3.1), it is profit-maximizing for the shop to charge the one retail price, p_0. From (3.5) and (3.7) the size of this range, labelled S, can be expressed as

$$S = (p^p_{min} / p^p_{max}) = \frac{(\eta + \mu)((1 + X)(\eta - 1) + \mu)}{(\eta + \mu - 1)(1 + X)\eta + \mu}$$ (3.8)

From (3.8) the range of price, S, is a position function of X. Furthermore, dX/dT is positive because $dX/dT = (c(p_0)/c(p))r(e^{rT} - 1 - rT)/(e^{rT} + e^{-rT} - 2) > 0$ since, by application of Taylor's theorem, $e^{rT} - 1 - rT = (rT)^2/2! + (rT)^3/3! + \ldots > 0$. Thus the lower the frequency of search by customers the larger is the range between p^p_{min} and p^p_{max}.

3.3   Profit-maximizing Behaviour by a Shop Selling Many Types of Goods

Assume that a shop sells g types of good. Define the row vector of the prices of the g goods as

$$p = \{p_1, p_2, \ldots, p_g\}$$ (3.9)

Assume that each customer is identical, and define the set of shares of expenditure devoted to each good as the column vector

$$\sigma = \{\sigma_1, \sigma_2, \ldots, \sigma_g\}$$ (3.10)

where $\sum_{i=1}^{g} \sigma_i = 1$. Then the price index of the basket of goods purchased by each customer is $p\sigma$. For the many-good case, the function determining the long-run size of the clientele is written $c(p\sigma)$, with $c'(p\sigma) < 0$.

Each customer has a set of demand functions

$$\mathbf{h} = \begin{bmatrix} h_1(\mathbf{p}) \\ h_2(\mathbf{p}) \\ \vdots \\ h_g(\mathbf{p}) \end{bmatrix} \tag{3.11}$$

To avoid corner solutions the demand functions are restricted by

$$\mathbf{p} > 0 \qquad \text{implies} \qquad h_i > 0 \qquad \text{for } i = 1, \dots, g$$

This restriction is discussed below. The revenue flow of a shop is

$$c(\mathbf{p\sigma})\mathbf{ph} \tag{3.12}$$

and the flow of costs is

$$c(\mathbf{p\sigma})\mathbf{p}^p\mathbf{h} + F \tag{3.13}$$

where $\mathbf{p}^p$ is the row vector of the producer prices of the g goods.

If the firm maintains or raises any of its retail prices then the discounted sum of profits is simply

$$\Pi^+ = \int_{t=0}^{\infty} \{c(\mathbf{p\sigma})(\mathbf{p} - \mathbf{p}^p)\mathbf{h} - F\}e^{-rt}\mathrm{d}t \tag{3.14}$$

On the other hand, if the shop lowers any of its retail prices then, allowing for the customer build-up period, the discounted sum of profits is

$$\Pi^- = \int_{t=0}^{T} \{c_t(\mathbf{p} - \mathbf{p}^p)\mathbf{h} - F\}e^{-rt}\mathrm{d}t + \int_{t=T}^{\infty} \{c(\mathbf{p\sigma})(\mathbf{p} - \mathbf{p}^p)\mathbf{h} - F\}e^{-rt}\mathrm{d}t \tag{3.15}$$

where c_t is determined by (3.1a). For the jth good the shopkeeper's problem is to choose p_j to maximize either (3.14) or (3.15), whichever is the greater. The first-order condition for maximizing Π^+ by choice of p_j can be written

$$p_j \frac{\mu_j + [\mathbf{p}\eta_j\mathbf{h} - h_j(\mathbf{p})p_j](1/R)}{\mu_j + [\mathbf{p}^p\eta_j\mathbf{h}/R^p](R^p/R)} = p_j^p \tag{3.16}$$

where

$$\mu_j = \frac{-\partial c(\mathbf{p\sigma})}{\partial p_j}\frac{p_j}{c(\mathbf{p\sigma})}, \qquad \eta_j = \begin{bmatrix} \eta_{1j} & 0 & ... & 0 \\ 0 & \eta_{2j} & ... & 0 \\ . & . & . & . \\ 0 & 0 & ... & \eta_{gj} \end{bmatrix}$$

$$\eta_{ij} = \frac{-\partial h_i(p)}{\partial p_j}\frac{p_j}{h_i(\mathbf{p})}, \qquad R = \mathbf{ph}, \qquad R^p = \mathbf{p}^p\mathbf{h}$$

The first-order condition for maximizing Π by choice of p_j can be written as

$$p_j \frac{\mu_j + [\mathbf{p}\eta_j\mathbf{h} - p_jh_j(\mathbf{p})](1+X)/R}{\mu_j + [\mathbf{p}^p\eta_j\mathbf{h}(1+X)/R^p](R^p/R)} = p_j^p \qquad (3.17)$$

There is a step in the marginal revenue function from sales of the jth good, similar to the one-good case. The step is

$$S_j = (p_{j\min}^p/p_{j\max}^p)$$
$$= \left\{ \frac{\mu_j + [\mathbf{p}\eta_j\mathbf{h} - p_jh_j(\mathbf{p})](1+X)/R}{\mu_j + \mathbf{p}^p\eta_j\mathbf{h}(1+X)/R^p} \right\} \Big/ \left\{ \frac{\mu_j + [\mathbf{p}\eta_j\mathbf{h} - p_jh_j(\mathbf{p})]/R}{\mu_j + \mathbf{p}^p\eta_j\mathbf{h}/R^p} \right\}$$

$$(3.18)$$

If either $\mu_j = 0$ or $h_j(\mathbf{p}) = 0$ then the step disappears (that is, $\mu_j = 0$ or $h_j(\mathbf{p}) = 0$ imply $S_j = 1$). The condition $\mu_j = 0$ implies that the size of the clientele is unaffected by changes in p_j, effectively ruling out the asymmetric dynamics of the determination of the size of the clientele. $h_j(\mathbf{p}) = 0$ means that good j is not sold. This possibility is ruled out by the restriction placed on the customers' demand functions (3.11). Assuming $\mu_j > 0$ and $h_j(\mathbf{p}) > 0$, then if $X > 0$, the condition for $S_j < 1$ is

$$\sum_{i=1}^{g} \eta_{ij}(\sigma_i - \sigma_i^p) < \sigma_j \qquad (3.19)$$

where

$$\sigma_i = p_ih_i(\mathbf{p})/R, \qquad \sigma_i^p = p_i^ph_i(\mathbf{p})/R^p$$

and it is assumed that the sign of $\mu_j + \mathbf{p}^p\eta_j\mathbf{h}(1 + X)/R^p$ is the same as the sign of $\mu_j + \mathbf{p}^p\eta_j\mathbf{h}/R^p$.

Condition (3.19) is a weak condition because it is reasonable, for two reasons, to think of the left-hand side as approximately zero. The shares σ_i and σ_i^p are proportions of expenditure accounted for by good i at retail prices and at wholesale prices respectively. Even if they are not equal, these shares are likely to be very close. Furthermore, for goods which are substitutes, the own-price and cross-price elasticities will have opposite signs and so tend to cancel out (this is commented on below). However, although weak, it is worth contrasting this condition with the one-good case. With a retailer selling one good, $X > 0$ is sufficient to generate a step (S, given by equation (3.8)) in the marginal revenue function.

3.4   The Determination of Producer Prices

The determination of producer prices depends on the power of producers relative to that of retailers. We consider first the case in which the producer is a price-maker, setting the producer price for a particular good. Then we consider the impact of allowing for some monopsony power by retailers and of competition between producers.

For the case of the price-setting producer assume there are g producers. Each good is produced by only one producer and each producer produces only one type of good. Each producer offers his good to all of the retailers. To analyse the response of purchases by retailers to changes in the producer price, consider figure 3.2.

In figure 3.2, y^d is the long-run demand curve for a particular good, j, facing a particular retailer, derived under the assumption that all other retailers are holding their retail prices fixed. Along y^d the size of the retailer's clientele will vary. The marginal revenue curve in figure 3.2 is derived by combining y^d with the asymmetric dynamics of clientele size that arise in a customer market. Because of these asymmetric dynamics, the marginal revenue curve has a discontinuity at the level of sales $y_{j,0}$. In the derivation of the marginal revenue curve in figure 3.2, the retailer is assumed to believe that all other retailers are holding their retail

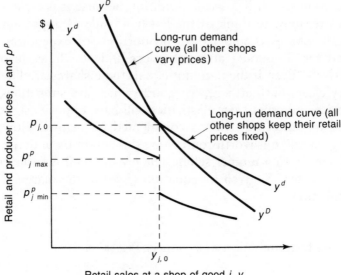

Figure 3.2

prices constant. Given this belief, the retailer will alter the retail price only if the producer price is set outside the range of $p^p_{j\,min}$ to $p^p_{j\,max}$.

Now suppose that the producer raises the producer price of good j above $p^p_{j\,max}$. Assume that all retailers have identical demand curves and marginal revenue curves. Under the belief that all other retailers are maintaining their prices, the retailer will raise the retail price. because all retailers raise their retail price of good j, each retailer will experience a change in sales according to y^D in figure 3.2. Along y^D, all retailers are changing their prices and so there will be little, if any, change in the size of the clienteles of individual retailers. Those customers induced to search by the increase in retail price will find a similar increase at other retailers, and will presumably drift back to their original shop. Sales of good j will decline in as much as customers switch to substitute goods. The elasticity of this response of sales, that is the elasticity of y^D, is η_{jj}, the own-price elasticity. This elasticity can be fairly large if retailers stock close substitutes of the good j.

To induce a decline in the retail price, the producer price has to be set below $p^p_{j\,\min}$. A reduction of the producer price to below $p^p_{j\,\min}$ will lead to a reduction in retail price and an increase in sales as customers switch away from substitutes to good j. The size of the reduction in retail prices is given by the own-price elasticity η_{jj}. Unlike the retailer, the producer does not have to wait for sales to rise following a cut in producer price which is sufficiently large to induce a cut in retail price. The producer is unaffected by competition between shops and is only concerned with competition between goods. A producer price below $p^p_{j\,\min}$ for all shops will induce all shops to cut retail price and will induce an immediate increase in the sales of this good at all shops, a decrease in the sales of substitutes and, in our model, no change to the number of customers patronizing each shop.

This analysis of the effect on sales of variations in producer price implies the demand curve and marginal revenue curve facing a producer shown in figure 3.3. Both the demand curve and the marginal revenue curve have a discontinuity. The price-setting producer of good j will set a price equal to $p^p_{j\,\max}$ as long as the producer's marginal cost curve passes through the discontinuity in the producer's marginal revenue curve. Shifts of the marginal cost curve outside this range will induce the producer to change the producer price from $p^p_{j\,\max}$, and induce an immediate adjustment of purchases of the good by retailers and customers.

For the above case, where the producer dominates the price-setting process, and where all retailers are identical, producer prices are set at $p^p_{j\,\max}$, and fluctuations in producer prices are of the same size as the fluctuations in retail prices. However, in the empirical evidence reviewed in chapter 4, fluctuations of producer prices are not the same as the observed fluctuations in retail prices.

If the assumption of identical shops is dropped, then a more realistic pattern of retail and producer price behaviour is generated. Assume that shops are not identical in that their values of $p^p_{j\,\max}$ differ. Assume that the producer charges the same producer price to all shops. This price-setting producer will no longer experience a vertical discontinuity in the demand curve for his product. There will be particular values of the producer price which will equal the $p^p_{j\,\max}$ for some shops, the $p^p_{j\,\min}$ for other shops

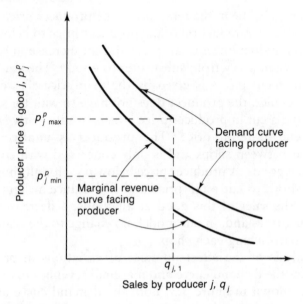

Figure 3.3

and lie between the $p^p_{j\,\text{max}}$ and $p^p_{j\,\text{min}}$ for the remaining shops. From such a producer price, a small change will induce some, but not all, shops to change their retail price. By inducing only a proportion of retailers to change their retail price for the good, these changes in the common producer price facing all retailers will induce small changes in the average retail price paid by consumers (the average being the average across retailers).

An example of this analysis is shown in figure 3.4. In the example, a producer is assumed to sell a particular good to three retailers. The j subscript, denoting the jth good, is dropped. Let y_i be producer sales to retailer i. The producer price of p^p_1 is equal to p^p_{max} for retailer 1, lies between p^p_{max} and p^p_{min} for retailer 2, and is equal to p^p_{min} for retailer 3. A small increase in producer price above p^p_1 will induce retailer 1 to increase her retail price, but will not induce the other two retailers to change their retail prices. A small decrease in producer price below p^p_1 will induce retailer 3 to reduce her retail price, but will not induce retailers 1 and 2 to change their retail prices. Fluctuations in the average retail price

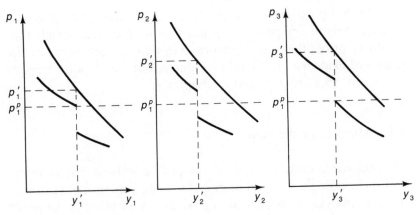

Figure 3.4

are damped by the existence of a discontinuity in the marginal revenue function.

In general, retailers may differ because of differences in both their cost functions and their demand functions. The analysis in this chapter has excluded, by assumption, from the costs of retailing all variable costs other than the cost of purchasing producer goods. To include these other costs of selling would allow for a further dimension of variation between retailers, giving an additional basis for the damping of fluctuations in retail prices.

The assumption that the producer has complete power to set price is extreme. Retailers may be able to bargain with producers and force the producer price below p^p_{max} by making an all-or-nothing offer. They may threaten not to stock a producer's good unless the producer sets a price which shares some of the rents from market power with the retailer: the closer the available substitutes, the more force will such a threat have. If we assume that a particular good is produced by several producers, then competition among these producers may force producer price down to marginal cost. In these cases, in which retailers have some influence over producer price, variations in the marginal cost of producing may lead to variations in producer price without inducing variations in any retail price.

Assuming that either retailers differ with regard to the value of

$p^p_{j\,\text{max}}$ or that producers compete in selling to retailers leads to the pattern of retail and producer prices that is observed, namely that producer prices fluctuate by more than retail prices. Some of the empirical evidence on the relative fluctuations of producer prices and retail prices is reviewed in chapter 4.

3.5   The Size of the Step

The macroeconomic models developed in subsequent chapters will show how the stepped marginal revenue function of customer market analysis is a crucial ingredient in yielding a range of equilibrium levels of aggregate employment. To help to assess the significance of these models, the size of the range of equilibrium is calculated using reasonable parameter values. Reasonable sizes for the step in the demand function can be calculated as follows.

Equation (3.18) relates the size of the step to a number of parameters. The sum $p\eta_j h$ combines the offsetting effects of a large positive own-price elasticity with the large negative cross-price elasticities of close substitutes. It is reasonable to assume that income effects are negligible for individual items. If income effects are negligible then the sum $p\eta_j h$ can be approximated to zero. On these ground $p^p\eta_j h$ can also be set to zero. With these sums set to zero the equation for the step simplifies to

$$S_j = \frac{\mu_j - (1 + X)\sigma_j}{\mu_j - \sigma_j} \tag{3.20}$$

where $\sigma_j = p_j h_j(\mathbf{p})/R$.

From the function determining the size of a shop's clientele, $c(\mathbf{p\sigma})$, the elasticity, μ_j, can be written as

$$\mu_j = \mu p_j \sigma_j / \mathbf{p\sigma}$$

where $\mu = c'(\mathbf{p})\mathbf{p}/c(\mathbf{p})$. Multiplying the top and bottom of the right-hand side by R,

$$\mu_j = \mu p_j h_j(\mathbf{p})/\mathbf{ph}$$

Therefore

$$\mu_j = \mu\sigma_j \qquad (3.21)$$

Substituting (3.21) into (3.20), the step is given by

$$S_j = \frac{\mu - (1 + X)}{\mu - 1} \qquad (3.22)$$

Under these simplifying assumptions, all goods sold by the shop have marginal revenue curves with a step of the same size. Whatever their individual price elasticity, only the dynamics of the number of customers matter. This is a rather surprising result. Two comments should be made. First, the restriction on the demand functions (3.11) rules out price elasticities of infinity. With perfect substitutes, tiny variations in price could cause sales of one good to fall to zero. The result would be a corner solution which is beyond the mathematical analysis presented here. Second, the simplifications embodied in equation (3.22) rule out characteristics which could yield different-sized steps for different goods. For example, in practice some goods may have the potential to attract customers beyond their relative importance in consumers' expenditure plans: for those goods $\mu_j > \mu\sigma_j$. This loss of detail will have little impact on the average step across all goods sold by a store and so (3.22) is suitable for our purposes.

The size of the step given by equation (3.22) is based on the assumption that $p\eta_j h = 0$. This assumption allows the own-price elasticity and cross-price elasticities to differ from zero. It is their weighted sum which is assumed to equal zero. In the model of a shop selling only one good, setting the own-price elasticity at zero ($\eta = 0$) reduces the expression determining the size of the step (the right-hand side of (3.8)) to the same expression as the right-hand side of (3.22). A customer at a shop selling only one good can only substitute another good by changing to another shop. Given that the opportunity of substitutes is not available without switching to another shop, the reasonable assumption for a value of η is close to zero. Thus equation (3.22) emerges as the reasonable guide to the size of the step for both the multi-good shop and the one-good shop.

Three parameters enter equation (3.22): r, T and μ. The sizes of the step S_j for a range of values of these parameters are compar-

Table 3.1 Values of the step in the demand function facing suppliers to shops

μ	$p^p_j/p^p_{j\,min}$	0.05	0.1	0.2	0.3
			rT		
1.5	0.33	0.9496	0.8983	0.7933	0.6850
2	0.5	0.9748	0.9492	0.8967	0.8425
3	0.67	0.9874	0.9746	0.9483	0.9213
4	0.75	0.9916	0.9831	0.9656	0.9475
5	0.8	0.9937	0.9873	0.9742	0.9606

ed in table 3.1. There is no good empirical evidence about T, the length of time over which a consumer, with no special stimulus, checks the prices of all potential suppliers. A reasonable guess would be between 6 months and several years. In table 3.1 the range of rT from 0.05 to 0.3 encompasses a 10 per cent discount rate with T ranging from 6 months to 3 years, or a 5 per cent discount rate with T ranging from 1 to 6 years. The size of the margin between retail prices and wholesale prices can give some guidance to reasonable values of μ. The second column in table 3.1 reports the value of $p_j/p^p_{j\,max}(=(\mu-1)/\mu))$ implied by the value of μ in column one. The margins observed for supermarkets would suggest a value of μ of 5: for other stores lower values of μ would probably apply, although values below 2 would be rare. Applying these values of r, T and μ gives a range of values of the step between 0.9 and 0.99.

3.6 Aggregate Demand and Employment

The existence of a step in the marginal revenue curve of retailers leads to the result that a change in the nominal level of aggregate demand can alter the equilibrium level of real output of the economy. Nominal changes can have permanent real effects. This proposition can be demonstrated more easily for the case in which producer prices are determined competitively than for the case where the producer is a price-maker. Furthermore, this case is not only easier but is also consistent with the empirical evidence reviewed in chapter 4. It is the case discussed in subsequent chapters. Therefore, in the demonstration that follows of the impact of changes in the nominal level of aggregate demand on real activity, producer prices are assumed to be determined competitively.

Consider an expansion in the nominal level of aggregate demand. Shops will experience a shift to the right in their demand curves. At the initial retail price, sales will increase and the step in the marginal revenue curve will shift to the right. A general increase in sales by shops across the economy will raise the sales of producers. This will tend to put upward pressure on producer prices for a number of reasons. If wages are set competitively so that the economy is at full employment, then producers will have to pay higher real wages (money wages deflated by *retail* prices) to induce the increase in the supply of labour necessary to produce extra output. An increase in the real producer price, the producer price relative to the retail price, will encourage producers to increase production. Even in a non-competitive labour market, in which real wages are set by some mechanism other than a market-clearing one, an expansion in employment may still require an increase in real wages, yielding a similar pressure on producer prices as in the case of a competitive labour market. Furthermore, in either a competitive or non-competitive labour market the existence of diminishing returns to labour will place upward pressure on producer prices when there is an increase in the demand for the output produced by producers.

With retailers selling in customer markets, the existence of a vertical section in their marginal revenue curves allows the possibility that producer prices can increase relative to retail prices. An increase in demand can lead to an increase in producer prices relative to retail prices. Obviously, the argument can work in reverse for a fall in aggregate demand. Thus a change in the nominal level of aggregate demand can change the ratio of retail prices to producer prices.

The macroeconomic effect of a change in the ratio of retail prices to producer prices is illustrated in figure 3.5. The aggregate supply of labour to producers, L^s, is shown as a positive function

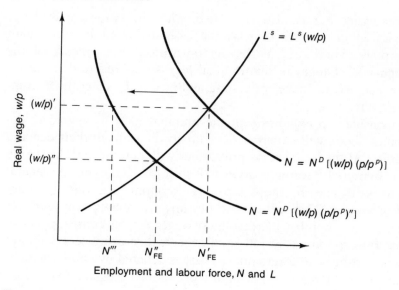

Figure 3.5

of the consumer real wage, the money wage deflated by the retail price. The aggregate demand for labour by producers is a negative function of the producer real wage, that is the money wage deflated by the producer price. With perfectly competitive producers, this labour demand curve is the aggregate marginal product of labour schedule for producers. To show the aggregate demand curve for labour in figure 3.5, the producer wage is expressed as a function of the consumer wage by multiplying it by the ratio of retail price to producer price; that is, $w/p^p = (w/p)(p/p^p)$. Changes in the ratio p/p^p will shift the labour demand curve: for example, a decline in p/p^p will shift the labour demand curve to the left. This example is shown in figure 3.5.

The proposition that a change in the nominal level of aggregate demand can lead to a change in the equilibrium level of real output can be demonstrated as follows. A decline in aggregate demand shifts the demand curves facing retailers to the left. Sales decline at constant retail prices, reducing demand for producers' goods. This puts downward pressure on producer prices, shifting the demand for labour curve in figure 3.5 to the left. Provided that at the lower producer prices the retailers' marginal cost curves continue to cut the retailers' marginal revenue curves within the step, the labour demand curve will remain at its depressed level. The exact point at which the level of employment will settle depends on the adjustment in real wages. If wages are determined by competitive forces then they will be bid down by the decline in demand, and employment in figure 3.5 would adjust from the full employment level, N'_{FE}, to the lower full employment level, N''_{FE}. If real wages are rigid at the level $(w/p)'$ then employment will decline to N''' and there will be involuntary unemployment.

The macroeconomic models developed in chapters 5–8 are variations on the analysis of figure 3.5. The variations reflect different assumptions about how the real wage is determined. In each of chapters 5–8, mechanisms which lead to real wages above market-clearing levels are presented, and a range of equilibrium levels of involuntary unemployment is derived.

3.7 Conclusion

This chapter has presented the theory of the determination of retail prices in a customer market by a shop selling many types of goods. The marginal revenue curve from the sales of each good was shown to have a discontinuity. Under reasonable assumptions, the size of this discontinuity depends only on the customer dynamics and is independent of own-price and cross-price elasticities.

The model has concentrated on allowing for many types of goods to be sold. This concentration leaves other aspects relatively underdeveloped. In particular, a more sophisticated modelling of the ways in which customers acquire information about the prices charged by competing suppliers would appear to warrant attention. For a recent paper which models the acquisition of information by customers, see Sibly (1988). Other extensions would allow for advertising and for variable price strategies.

4 Empirical Evidence on Customer Markets

Using the theory of price behaviour in a customer market set out in the previous chapter, this chapter shows how the existence of a customer market can be inferred from data on prices. The main focus of attention is on the empirical analysis in McDonald and Spindler (1987).

The basic hypothesis of a customer market has been developed and investigated empirically by agricultural economists, particularly within Australia. The Australian tradition has concentrated on the pricing behaviour of meat retailers and wholesalers. The basic theoretical contribution to this literature is Parish (1966), who argues that retailers of meat will both 'average' and 'level' retail prices if they sell to a stable clientele. In empirical studies, the evidence tends to support the idea that meat retailers average and level prices. In the next section the Australian literature is reviewed briefly.

4.1 A Brief Review of Australian Studies of Customer Markets

To explain the inverse relationship often observed between prices and farm–wholesale or farm–retail margins (see, for example, Williams and Stout, 1964; Kohls and Uhl, 1980), Parish (1966) developed the idea of an asymmetric demand response to changes in price. Parish divided buyers into regular customers, who tend to patronize a particular shop, and comparison shoppers, who search all competing shops before making their purchases. Parish argued that the existence of regular customers brings greater stability to retail prices. Two stabilizing mechanisms can distinguished: averaging, in which retailers spread their costs across all classes of goods sold in order to minimize the extent of an individual price change; and levelling, which occurs when margins are varied to smooth retail prices over time in the face of fluctuating wholesale prices.

Using quarterly data for fresh beef, lamb and mutton in the New South Wales livestock auction, wholesale and retail markets, Marceau (1967) found that auction-to-wholesale and wholesale-to-retail margins varied inversely with movements in the auction price. The compression of the structure of prices when auction prices rose was attributed by Marceau (1967, p. 61) to the costs involved in altering prices and to the desire of firms not to alienate their customers by too frequent price changes. Griffith (1974) extended Marceau's work by using monthly data from New South Wales on beef, lamb, mutton and pork prices, and estimating a simultaneous equation system to allow for interdependence between the demands for various types of meats. He also allowed for a dynamic structure by using both current and lagged prices as explanatory variables. The results of Griffith's study support the hypothesis that short-run price levelling occurs.

Naughtin and Quilkey (1979) and Naughtin (1977) developed a theoretical model of a multi-product shop selling in a customer market. Naughtin and Quilkey investigated the implications of their model using data on retail revenue and on expenditure on the purchase of goods from wholesalers for three butchers in the Melbourne metropolitan area. They found that not only did butchers average and level retail prices, but also that these practices were not confined to a planning horizon of three months.

Watson and Parish (1982, p. 338) concluded that 'The existence of both levelling and averaging has been confirmed in empirical studies of the Australian meat market'. Since it is not just meat retailers but most sellers of frequently purchased items who sell in customer markets, the price stickiness predicted by customer market analysis should be apparent not only for meat but other goods as well.

4.2 Formulating a Test for the Existence of a Customer Market

The important conclusion to be drawn from the analysis of customer markets is that there is a range over which wholesale price can vary without the shopkeeper varying retail price. Consider an initial situation in which marginal cost equals marginal revenue at the top of the step. Disturb this initial situation by making a small reduction in wholesale price. If the lowered wholesale price has not reduced marginal cost to an amount less than marginal revenue at the foot of the step, there is no incentive for the shopkeeper to cut retail price. A cut in retail price will be profit-maximizing for the shopkeeper only when marginal cost has fallen to less than the value of marginal revenue at the foot of the step. In more general terms, changes in costs will only affect price if they are large enough to move the marginal cost curve outside the step of the marginal revenue curve.

The invariance of price to those changes in cost which leave the marginal cost curve intersecting the step in the marginal revenue curve is not temporary. The step does not disappear over time. Whenever a shopkeeper considers the retail price to set, she has to take into account the dynamics of the number of customers. A reduction in retail price, whenever made, will be followed by a customer build-up period.

In the empirical investigations reported in the next section, data on market prices are studied. Define the index of retail prices for a market (RP) as

$$RP = \sum_{i=1}^{z} \zeta_i p_i \qquad (4.1)$$

where z is the number of shops in the market, ζ_i is the share of the sales of shop i in the total sales for the market (so that $\sum_{i=1}^{z} \zeta_i = 1$) and p_i is the retail price of shop i.

In this definition of the retail price index, p_i can be thought of as the retail price of a particular good sold by shop i or an index of a basket of goods sold by shop i. Of course, the same choice between these alternatives has to be made for all shops. This choice then determines the coverage over goods of the market index RP.

If all shops in a market were identical in their cost and demand structures, the index of retail prices might be expected to behave in a discontinuous fashion: that is, within the limits set by equations (3.5) and (3.7) in chapter 3, fluctuations in wholesale price would not affect the index of retail prices. At the limits set by equations (3.5) and (3.7) the index of retail prices would move with the index of wholesale prices. However, in general, shops will have different marginal revenue and marginal cost curves. Imagine that for those shops the prices of which comprise the retail price index, the intersection points of marginal cost with marginal revenue range over the step. For some shops, marginal cost will cut at the top of the marginal revenue step. For others, marginal cost will cut marginal revenue at the foot of the step. For the remaining shops, the intersections of marginal cost and marginal revenue will be spread throughout the step. Furthermore, assume that the elasticities, μ and η, the discount rate, r, and the time span, T, are constant. A change in the marginal cost for all shops in the market will affect the retail prices of only some shops and so may be expected to cause a smaller change in the index of retail prices. For example, if costs of all shops increase, then the marginal cost curves of only some shops will be pushed above the marginal revenue step, inducing those shops only to raise their prices. The index of retail prices will increase by a proportion of the increase in marginal cost, where the proportion is equal to the share in total market sales of sales by shops the marginal cost curves of which are pushed above the step in their marginal revenue curves. With this proportion less than one, a 1 per cent increase in marginal cost at all shops will lead to a less than 1 per cent increase in the index of retail prices. A similar argument applies to the effect on the retail price index of decreases in marginal cost: that is, a general fall in marginal costs will push the marginal cost curves of some shops only below the step in their marginal revenue curves. The other shops will not reduce their retail prices and so the fall in the index of retail prices will be damped. In the standard economic model in which the marginal revenue curve is continuous, a 1 per cent change in marginal cost leads to a 1 per cent change in retail prices if the elasticity of the demand curve is constant. In a customer market a 1 percent change in marginal costs can lead to a less than 1 per cent change in the index of retail prices, even if the elasticities of the demand curve, μ and η, are constant. Therefore, if an elasticity of the index of retail prices with respect to marginal cost of less than one is observed, then the existence of a customer market may be inferred.

The constant-elasticity version of the standard economic model is a reasonable benchmark by which to judge whether the flexibility of retail prices is low, which would suggest the existence of a customer market. While the constant-elasticity case may appear to be a rather special version of the standard economic model, low flexibility of retail prices can only be explained by that model if the elasticity of the demand curve varies systematically with changes in marginal costs. In particular, the elasticity of the demand curve would have to increase with *any* change, positive or negative, in marginal cost. The inference of the existence of a customer market is based on the assumption that the elasticity of demand does not vary systematically with marginal cost.

In the empirical investigation reviewed in the next section, data on wholesale prices are used. The cost of wholesale goods is the major component of shops' marginal costs. For example, Douglas (1962, table 3) presents figures for the USA in 1956/7 for 14 groups of retail food corporations classified by size, ranging from those with assets of less than $25000 (group 1) to those with assets of $250000 or more (group 14). For these groups, the percentage of marginal cost accounted for by the cost of wholesale goods was about 80 per cent. In a study of a large multi-output retailer in the UK, Tucker (1975, p. 101) reports that the cost of wholesale goods accounted for 80 per cent of variable costs. So, in the standard economic model, the elasticity of retail price with respect to wholesale price would be expected to be about 0.8. Therefore, if the measured elasticity is significantly less than 0.8 there is some evidence of a customer market.

Going beyond the basic model as specified above, retail prices would be expected to move with shopkeepers' guesses concerning their customers' perceptions about movements in the prices of retail goods at competing shops. In an inflationary environment it is reasonable to assume that customers expect shops to raise their prices at the rate of inflation. If customers do indeed have such expectations, than an increase in the retail prices of the shop they patronize in line with the rate of inflation will not induce them to search out other suppliers. Therefore, in a customer market, retail prices can be expected to increase with the expected rate of inflation.

In the basic model, it is assumed that shops have a constant returns to scale technology. If this assumption does not hold, then shopkeepers may change retail prices when their demand curves shift. For example, if shops have increasing returns to scale technologies, as is often suggested in the literature (see, for example, Tucker, 1975) then increases in demand may reduce retail prices. In a customer market the existence of stepped marginal revenue curves will weaken the size of this effect. In the statistical analysis in McDonald and Spindler (1987) the possibility of non-constant returns to scale is allowed for by including a proxy for the level of demand. The proxy selected was the percentage change in real aggregate consumption expenditure.

In general, a gradual adjustment of retail prices might be expected because decision-makers (shopkeepers) will react with a recognition lag and an action lag when the economic environment changes. The action lag of retailers operating in customer markets may be longer than for other markets because of a stronger than usual concern not to upset customers. To allow for the possibility of gradual adjustment of retail prices, lagged values of the wholesale price variable and the demand variable were incorporated into the estimating equation. Since the discontinuity in the marginal revenue curve implied by customer market analysis does not disappear over time, long-run effects on retail prices must be examined to appraise the evidence for customer markets.

These considerations about the determination of retail prices suggest the following general estimating equation:

$$rp = \alpha_0 + \alpha_1 wp + \alpha_2 ei + \alpha_3 rc + \text{lags} \qquad (4.2)$$

where *rp* is the percentage change in the retail price index, *wp* is the percentage change in the wholesale price index, *ei* is the expected annual inflation rate and *rc* is the percentage change in real aggregate consumption expenditure. The constant term is included to allow for the possibility that a persistent difference between the growth of factor productivity in retailing relative to the rest of the economy will induce a persistent difference in the change of retail prices relative to wholesale prices.

4.3 A Review of the Evidence

In McDonald and Spindler (1987) a number of price indexes are investigated for evidence of the existence of a customer market. For the USA, the UK and Australia, aggregate retail price indexes and food retail price indexes are matched with wholesale price indexes and producer price indexes. In addition, retail price indexes of individual meats (lamb, beef and pork) for Sydney, Australia are matched with indexes of saleyard prices.

The analysis presented earlier suggests that in a customer market, retail prices fluctuate by less than wholesale prices. A preliminary test of this hypothesis is the comparison of the standard deviation of the percentage changes in a retail price index with the standard deviation of the percentage changes in the corresponding wholesale price index. The standard deviations for all data series on retail and wholesale prices used in McDonald and Spindler (1987) are presented in table 4.1. In every case except one the standard deviation of the percentage change in retail prices is smaller than the standard deviation of the percentage change in the corresponding wholesale price index. This behaviour is consistent with the existence of customer markets.

In the regression analysis in McDonald and Spindler (1987), equation (4.2) above is estimated. The estimates of the long-run value of α_1, the coefficient on wholesale (or producer where relevant) price, are presented in table 4.2. From the studies of Douglas (1962) and Tucker (1975) cited earlier, the cost of wholesale goods appears to be about 80 per cent of retailers' marginal costs. This means that the existence of a customer mar-

Table 4.1   Standard deviations of retail and wholesale price movements

| | Standard deviations of | |
	%ΔRPI	%ΔWPI
Aggregate price indexes		
USA	0.95	1.32
UK	1.76	1.87
Australia	1.27	1.95
Food price indexes		
USA	1.51	2.70[a]
		4.54[b]
UK	2.48	2.24[a]
		6.14[b]
Australia	2.09	3.56
Individual meat product price indexes, Australia		
Lamb	12.49	23.02
Beef	9.09	22.99
Pork	9.77	16.29

[a] Wholesale price index for manufactured or processed food.
[b] Wholesale price index for agricultural products.
For data sources, see McDonald and Spindler (1987).

Table 4.2   Long-run value of the coefficient on the wholesale price index

Country	Time period	Coefficient	Standard error
General price indexes			
USA	1957(ii)–1983(ii)	0.166[ab]	0.042
UK	1957(ii)–1982(ii)	0.609[ab]	0.099
Australia	1960(ii)–1983(iii)	0.046[b]	0.045
Australia	1969(ii)–1983(iii)	0.189[b]	0.108
Food price indexes			
USA	1957(ii)–1979(ii)	0.553[ab]	0.063
UK	1957(ii)–1982(ii)	0.413[ab]	0.088
Australia	1970(iv)–1982(iii)	0.456[ab]	0.077

[a] Different from zero at the 95% level of significance.
[b] Less than 0.8 at the 95% level of significance.
For data sources, see McDonald and Spindler (1987).

Table 4.3 Long-run value of the coefficient on the wholesale price index of farm products.

Country	Time period	Coefficient	Standard error
USA	1958(iii)–1979(iii)	0.298[ab]	0.041
UK	1969(iii)–1982(ii)	0.316[a]	0.106
Australia	1960(ii) –1968(ii)	0.239[ab]	0.066

[a] Different from zero at the 95% level of significance.
[b] Less than 0.4 at the 95% level of significance.
For data sources, see McDonald and Spindler (1987).

ket can be inferred if the coefficient from regressions of retail prices on wholesale prices is significantly less than 0.8. The first seven rows of table 4.2 report the coefficients. The first four rows show coefficients estimated from general price indexes for the USA, the UK and Australia, and rows five to seven show coefficients estimated for food price indexes for the USA, the UK and Australia. As the crosses indicate, in every case the coefficient is less than 0.8, supporting the existence of customer markets at the 95 per cent level of significance.

In table 4.3 estimates from regressing retail price indexes of food on the wholesale price indexes of agricultural products are reported. The long-run value of the coefficient on the wholesale price, as well as the standard error, are reported. For these regressions it is appropriate to compare the wholesale price coefficient with the share of agricultural commodities in retailers' marginal costs. According to Kohls and Uhl (1980, p. 235), the farmer's share of the consumer's dollar has been generally in excess of 40 per cent in the USA in the period since the Second World War, and so the share of agricultural commodities in retailers' costs must be at least 40 per cent. Therefore, in table 4.3 estimates of the coefficient on the wholesale price of agricultural products which are significantly less than 0.4 are evidence that supports the existence of customer markets. As reported in table 4.3, two of the three long-run coefficients on the wholesale prices of agricultural products are significantly less than 0.4. The long-run coefficient in the regression for the UK is not significantly less than 0.4. However,

Table 4.4 *Long run value of the coefficient on wholesale prices for individual meat products, Australia*

Meat	Coefficient	Standard error
Lamb	0.624[a]	0.074
Beef	0.41[ab]	0.057
Pork	0.180[b]	0.091

Each estimate is based on annual data over the time period 1957–78.
[a] Different from 0 at the 95% level of significance.
[b] Less than 0.75 at the 95% level of significance.
For data sources, see McDonald and Spindler (1987).

it is small enough to be significantly less than 0.5 and so does not provide strong evidence against the existence of customer markets.

Finally, consider the regressions on individual meat product price indexes for Australia, as reported in table 4.4. The critical figure with which the wholesale price coefficient must be compared is the share of wholesale meat in marginal cost for meat retailers in Australia. According to the Prices Justification Tribunal (1978, p. 91), purchase of wholesale meat accounts for at least 75 per cent of operating costs, so 0.75 was taken as the critical cost share. In table 4.4, two of the three coefficients are less than 0.75 at the 95 per cent level of significance. The third coefficient, that for lamb, is significantly less than 0.752. So the estimates based on the prices of individual meat give further support to the existence of customer markets.

4.4   Conclusion

In the empirical investigation reported above data on retail, wholesale and producer prices for the USA, the UK and Australia at various levels of aggregation were found to be consistent with the predictions of the customer market model. Two principal results were:

(1) In eight cases out of nine, the standard deviations of the

percentage changes in the retail price indexes were less than those of the percentage changes in the wholesale price indexes.

(2) The elasticity of retail prices with respect to wholesale prices in the long run was found to be less than the share of expenditure on wholesale goods in retailers' variable costs.

These results are consistent with retailers absorbing some of the changes in wholesale prices so that changes in retail prices will not fully reflect the changes in wholesale prices. They are consistent with retailers having stepped marginal revenue curves, as in a customer market.

The relative volatility of wholesale and producer prices compared to retail prices shows up in significant variations in the ratio of retail prices to wholesale prices. For example, for the USA the general retail price index declined relative to the wholesale price index by 7 per cent between 1972 and 1974 and rose by 6 per cent between 1980 and 1983. Movements of similar size occur in Australia and the UK. This evidence suggests that values of the step in retailers' marginal revenue curves of around 0.95 are not unreasonable. This is in accord with the inferences drawn in the previous chapter from equation (3.22).

Part 3
Customer Markets, Efficiency Wages and the Range of Equilibria

5 Inducing Efficiency

In a customer market the unwillingness of customers to search before each purchase can lead to a discontinuity in the marginal revenue function facing suppliers. This chapter shows that when combined with wage-setting by producers to encourage effort, this discontinuity can yield a range of equilibrium levels of unemployment.

At present, models with a unique equilibrium dominate the macroeconomic literature. Models which exhibit ranges of macro-equilibria represent a radical departure. The existence of a range of macroeconomic equilibria opens up the possibility that the real level of activity in the economy can be increased (or decreased) without causing a persistent increase (or decrease) in the rate of inflation. The model described in this chapter is one example of a model with an equilibrium range. In chapters 6, 7 and 8 it is shown that customer market price-setting, combined with wage bargaining between a group of workers and an employer, can also yield a range of equilibrium rates of unemployment.

5.1 A Producing Firm with Efficiency Wage-setting

Assume that retailers, who sell in customer markets, buy goods from producers, who set wages with an eye to encouraging the effort of their employees on the lines put forward in the efficiency-wage theory (see Yellen, 1984; Shapiro and Stiglitz, 1984). Following the efficiency-wage approach, postulate that the efficiency of each employee is positively related to real wages in terms of consumer purchasing power, v, and negatively related to the flow per period of the real value of income receipts if laid off, $\bar{v}$. The derivation of $\bar{v}$ is presented later. The efficiency function is written as

$$e = e(v,\bar{v}), \quad e_v > 0, e_{\bar{v}} < 0, \quad e(v,\bar{v}) = 0 \text{ at } v = \hat{v} > 0 \qquad (5.1)$$

where $\hat{v}$ is a particular value of v.

For developed economies, Yellen (1984) places into four categories the various reasons why payment of wages which are high relative to income if laid off can encourage a higher level of efficiency. If the benefits from working are higher, then this can discourage shirking, reduce turnover, attract a higher-quality job applicant and raise morale. Because this chapter is concerned with the macroeconomic implications of combining efficiency-wage theory with customer market analysis, the efficiency function is not derived explicitly from any particular microfoundation. Instead, the efficiency function is taken to be representative of these ideas.

Assume that efficiency enters the firm's production function as a multiplicative factor on employment n, so that

$$q = f(en), \quad f' > 0, \quad f'' < 0 \qquad (5.2)$$

where q is output. The producing firm sets its money wage, w, and employment, n, to maximize profits; that is,

$$\text{Max } \pi = p^p q - wn \qquad (5.3)$$

subject to

$$q = f(en), \quad e = e(v,\bar{v}), \quad v = w/p$$

where p^p is the producer price. It is assumed in (5.3) that competition between producers in selling to retailers is sufficiently strong for producers to regard the price they receive from retailers as fixed. The fact that the objective in (5.3) is the nominal value of profits does not introduce money illusion on the part of producers into the analysis. Although producers, like workers, are interested in the real value of profits, since the decisions of an individual producer will not affect the price level, maximizing the nominal value of profits will lead to the same decision as maximizing the real value of profits, irrespective of the general price level. That is, dividing both sides of (5.3) by the aggregate price level to generate an expression for the real value of profits will not affect the first-order conditions, whatever the level of prices in the aggregate.

The first-order conditions for (5.3) can be written as

$$p^p e f'(en) = w, \tag{5.4}$$

$$\frac{\partial e(v,\bar{v})}{\partial v} \frac{v}{e(v,\bar{v})} = 1 \tag{5.5}$$

Equation (5.4) sets the marginal revenue product of a natural unit of labour equal to the money wage. Condition (5.5) is well known from Solow (1979). It sets the elasticity of efficiency with respect to the consumer real wage (money wages deflated by the retail price) equal to unity.

The determination by equation (5.5) of the optimal value of the consumer real wage, v^*, is illustrated in figure 5.1. The elasticity of the efficiency function is equal to unity at the tangency of the efficiency function with a ray from the origin. The marginal revenue product of labour deflated by the consumer price, p, is shown in figure 5.2. This curve is the left-hand side of equation (5.4) deflated by p. The negative slope of this marginal revenue product of labour schedule reflects diminishing returns to efficiency units of labour as well as lower efficiency per unit of labour at lower real wages. As v falls towards $\hat{v}$ the declining level of efficiency takes over, yielding a vertical marginal revenue product of labour curve at $v = \hat{v}$. (Recall that in equation (5.1) at $v = \hat{v}$ the efficiency function determines a zero level of efficiency.) The optimal level of employment can be read off figure 5.2 by finding the point on the marginal revenue product of labour schedule at $v = v^*$.

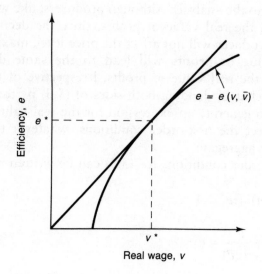

Figure 5.1

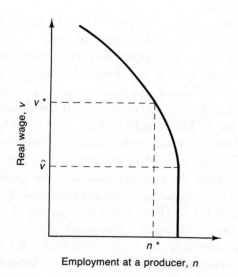

Figure 5.2

5.2 The Opportunity Cost of Labour

To embody the behaviour of an individual producer into a macro-economic model, the real value of income receipts if laid off, $\bar{v}$, has to be determined. The approach of Shapiro and Stiglitz (1984) is followed here to model the determination of $\bar{v}$. Assume a labour force of L people wishing to work for z producers. Assume that each producer has access to the same production technology and monitoring technology. Thus each producer has the same production function and effort function, and will pay the same real wage rate. Goods are retailed at many identical shops which, for ease of modelling, do not employ labour. We will concentrate on equilibria at which each shop charges the same retail price.

If unemployed, a worker faces a time of unemployment followed by a time of working at a new job. Unemployment time is spent searching and waiting (unemployment is involuntary) for a job. Assume that the probability that an unemployed worker will obtain a job in a period is $1/I$. Then a total of $(L - zn)/I$ jobs are acquired by the unemployed in each period. Assume that in each period zn/J vacancies are created. In equilibrium, the number of jobs acquired (vacancies filled) is equal to the number of vacancies created. By this condition,

$$\frac{1}{I} = \frac{zn}{(L-zn)J} \tag{5.6}$$

A job acquisition rate of $1/I$ implies that workers, on entering the pool if unemployed, face I periods of unemployment before getting a job. A job creation rate of $1/J$ implies that an employed worker can expect a job to last a further J periods. If unemployed, a worker can expect the present value of income payments over a time horizon of J periods to be

$$\int_0^I sv\,e^{-rt}\mathrm{d}t + \int_I^J v\,e^{-rt}\mathrm{d}t \tag{5.7}$$

where s represents the ratio of income from not working to the real wage. Income from not working is the sum of unemployment benefits plus the value of leisure if not working (that is, the disutility of work). Assuming that the ratio s is constant, equation (5.7) can be expressed as a constant flow per period, which is identified with $\bar{v}$. That flow is

$$\bar{v} = vG \tag{5.8}$$

where

$$G = 1 - (1-s)(1-e^{-rI})/(1-e^{-rJ}) \tag{5.9}$$

From (5.6), I can be expressed as a function of the aggregate employment ratio ($= E = zn/L$); that is,

$$I = ((1/E) - 1)/J \tag{5.10}$$

J is assumed to be exogenous to the model. Using (5.10), differentiation of (5.9) with respect to E yields

$$\partial G/\partial E = r(1-s)e^{-rI}/JE^2(1-e^{-rJ}) > 0 \tag{5.11}$$

The positive sign of $\partial G/\partial E$ shown by (5.11) implies, from (5.8), that for a given value of v, $\bar{v}$ is positively related to E. As one would expect, an increase in the aggregate employment ratio, at a particular value of the real wage, raises the value of the expected income flow of the unemployed. This is because an increase in the aggregate employment ratio reduces the length of time spent by the unemployed waiting for a job. Consequently, the real wage set by profit-maximizing entrepreneurs to induce the optimal amount of effort from their employees will also depend on the aggregate employment ratio.

By solving the five-equation system, (5.1), (5.5), (5.8), (5.9) and (5.10), the efficient value of the real wage can be shown to be a function of the aggregate employment ratio, E. To obtain an explicit expression for the relation between the efficient real wage and the aggregate employment ratio, assume the following specific functional form for the efficiency function:

$$e = v^\theta - \bar{v}^\phi, \quad 0 < \theta, \phi < 1 \tag{5.12}$$

from which the Solow condition (5.5) becomes

$$v^\theta(1-\theta) = \bar{v}^\phi \tag{5.13}$$

Using (5.13) in (5.8) yields

$$v = (1 - \theta)^{1/(\phi-\theta)} G^{\phi/(\theta-\phi)} \qquad (5.14)$$

For a given value of the aggregate employment ratio, E, (5.14) determines the real wage rate which optimizes the efficiency of employees. Equation (5.14) will be called the efficiency-wage schedule (EWS). From differentiation of (5.14) with respect to E, the slope of the EWS is

$$\frac{\partial v}{\partial E} = \frac{\phi(1-\theta)}{\theta-\phi}^{1/(\phi-\theta)} G^{(2\phi-\theta)/(\theta-\phi)} \frac{\partial G}{\partial E} \qquad (5.15)$$

From (5.15), the slope of the EWS depends on the sign of $\theta - \phi$. If θ is greater than ϕ then the schedule slopes upwards, implying a higher optimal wage as employment rises. This case has the appealing property that workers are induced to work more efficiently in a boom, agreeing with Hall's observation that 'Workers put in extra effort during booms and take it easy during slumps' (Hall, 1980, p. 95). To see this, substitute (5.8) and (5.14) into (5.11), yielding, after some rearrangement

$$e = G^{\phi\theta/(\theta-\phi)}[(1-\theta)^{\theta/(\phi-\theta)} - (1-\theta)^{\phi/(\phi-\theta)}] \qquad (5.16)$$

Differentiation of (5.16) with respect to E gives

$$\frac{\partial e}{\partial E} = \frac{\phi\theta}{(\theta-\phi)} G^{(\phi\theta-\theta+\phi)/(\theta-\phi)}[(1-\theta)^{\theta/(\phi-\theta)} - (1-\theta)^{\phi/(\phi-\theta)}] \frac{\partial G}{\partial E}$$

Clearly, $\partial e/\partial E > 0$ if $\theta > \phi$. The analagous curve to the EWS derived in Shapiro and Stiglitz (1984, p. 430), which they labelled the NSC (no-shirking constraint), is also upward-sloping. It will be assumed that $\theta > \phi$.

5.3 The Range of Macroeconomic Equilibria

To complete the macroeconomic model, assume that the z producers sell their output to a number of retailers. Each of these retailers sells goods to a pool of customers and sets the retail price along the lines of the theory of customer markets set out in chapter 3. The producers produce the same type of output, and competition between them forces the producer price down to the marginal cost of production. In the equilibria considered, all retailers set the same retail price. The real wage of those who work for producers is the nominal wage paid by producers deflated by the retail price.

Because of the assumption of a fixed number of identical producers, the efficiency-wage schedule can be drawn as a function of employment at a particular firm. Assuming that $\theta > \phi$, the EWS is upward-sloping, as shown above. Furthermore, as n approaches L/z, I approaches zero, $\partial G/\partial E$ approaches infinity (by 5.11) and the EWS becomes vertical. The EWS is shown in figure 5.3. Also shown in figure 5.3 is the marginal revenue product of labour schedule deflated by the retail price p.

The equation of the marginal revenue product of labour schedule is, deflating (5.4) by p,

$$\frac{p^p}{p} ef'(en) = v \tag{5.17}$$

For a given value of p^p/p, this schedule is downward-sloping, and becomes vertical at $v = \hat{v}$. An increase in the ratio p^p/p causes a clockwise rotation to the marginal revenue product of labour schedule above $\hat{v}$. An example of this rotation is shown in figure 5.3.

The intersection of the marginal revenue product of labour schedule with the efficiency-wage schedule determines the equilibrium level of employment. At this intersection the wage and employment decisions of the producers yield an aggregate employment ratio that is consistent with the individual producer's decisions. Because the EWS becomes vertical as n approaches L/z, that is as the employment ratio approaches one, the equilibrium level of employment is less than L/z. Therefore, in equilibrium there is involuntary unemployment. Without this involuntary unemployment there would be no differential between wages and the value of income receipts if laid off. Without a differential, the productivity of workers will be impaired. Firms would raise wages in an attempt to establish a differential with lay-off income. This differential can only exist if there is a pool of involuntary unemployment.

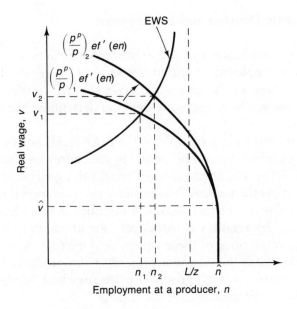

Figure 5.3

From figure 5.3, it is clear that a change in the ratio p^p/p will change the equilibrium levels of employment and unemployment. For example, an increase in p^p/p from $(p^p/p)_1$ to $(p^p/p)_2$ causes the marginal revenue product of labour schedule to increase in the direction shown by the arrow. The equilibrium level of employment increases from n_1 to n_2.

Under the standard theory of demand, in which marginal revenue curves are continuous, the ratio p^p/p is determined by the elasticity of demand. As discussed in chapter 2, this determines a unique equilibrium rate of unemployment. But with retailers selling in customer markets the ratio p^p/p is no longer uniquely determined. Instead, as the analysis of chapter 3 has shown, customer markets determine a range within which the ratio p^p/p must lie. Applying this range of p^p/p to the macroeconomic model represented in figure 5.3 determines a range of equilibrium levels of employment and an associated range of equilibrium rates of involuntary unemployment.

5.4   Aggregate Demand and Employment

An important implication of the existence of a range of equilibrium levels of employment is that the level of aggregate demand
determines where in the range the economy will settle. In this
section it is shown how aggregate demand determines the level of
employment.

In order to make clear the role of the price level, assume that a
particular value of the retail price, p_1 in figure 5.4, has been
established. At y_1, the actual level of retail sales generated by the
retail price, p_1, is the vertical discontinuity in the marginal revenue
curve. The existence of this discontinuity implies that changes in
the price paid by retailers to producers for goods may have no
effect on the retail price of these goods. Assume that the retailer's
only variable cost is the purchase of goods from producers. Then,
referring to figure 5.4, for a producer price anywhere between p^p_{min}
and p^p_{max}, the profit-maximizing retail price is p_1.

The impact on employment of changes in the level of aggregate
demand can be demonstrated with the aid of figures 5.5 and 5.6.
In figure 5.5, five demand curves facing a representative retailer
are shown. The five demand curves represent different levels of
aggregate demand. First consider demand curve y^d_2. Assume that a
retail price of p_1 has been established and that the vertical discontinuity in the marginal revenue curve (not shown) is at the level of
retail sales of y_2. In figure 5.5, five demand curves for labour to be
employed by a representative producer are shown. The EWS
drawn in figure 5.6 is contingent on a retail price of p_1. With a
producer price of p^p_{min} the labour demand curve is $w = p^p_{min} \, ef'(en)$.
This demand curve is shown as n^d_2 in figure 5.6 It cuts the EWS at
$\{w = w_2, n = n_2\}$. Assume that this is a macroeconomic equilibrium.
At a macroeconomic equilibrium the total output of goods, which
equals the number of producers times output per producer, has to
equal the total sales of goods, which equals the number of retailers
times sales per retailer. If q_2 is the output produced by n_2 workers
receiving a real wage of w_2/p_1 then, for a macroeconomic equilibrium, assume that zq_2 equals y_2 times the number of retailers. At
this macroeconomic equilibrium the producer price is p^p_{min}, the

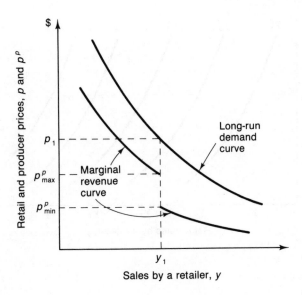

Figure 5.4

price at the foot of the vertical discontinuity in the retailer's marginal revenue curve. With a producer price of p^p_{min}, the profit-maximizing retailer sets a retail price of p_1.

Having set up this initial equilibrium, consider an increase in the level of nominal demand which shifts the demand curve facing the representative retailer to the right, to y^d_3 in figure 5.5. The vertical discontinuity in the retailer's marginal revenue curve is now at the level of retail sales of y_3. The total level of retail sales ($= y_3$ times the number of retailers) is equal to a level of production of zq_3. If producer price increases to p^p_3 then the labour demand curve, n^d_3, given by $w = p^p_3 \, ef'(en)$, cuts the EWS at n_3, the level of employment required to produce q_3 units of output. Because of diminishing returns to labour, producers require a higher producer price to produce the higher level of output of q_3. The discontinuity in their marginal revenue curves induces the profit-maximizing retailers to leave the retail price at p_1 even though they have to pay a higher producer price. That higher price, p^p_3, lies in the interval from p^p_{min} to p^p_{max}.

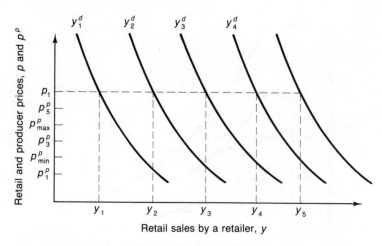

Figure 5.5

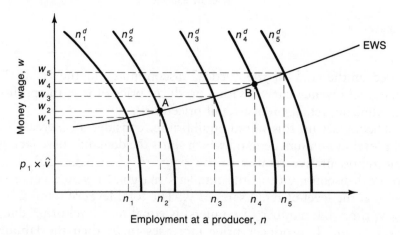

Figure 5.6

Consider an even higher level of demand which yields a demand curve facing the representative retailer of y_4^d. This can also yield a macroeconomic equilibrium. At this level of aggregate demand, the equilibrium level of employment at the representative producer is n_4. A producer price equal to p_{max}^p is required to induce producers to employ n_4 workers and produce q_4 output.

To induce a level of production in excess of q_4 requires a producer price in excess of $p_{\max}^p$. A producer price at this level will induce retailers to raise retail price. A rise in retail price will raise the EWS, pushing up the wage rate and the producer price. A macroequilibrium cannot be derived for levels of employment greater than n_4.

For levels of employment below n_2, a macroequilibrium does not exist. A retail demand curve of y_1^d will push the producer price below $p_{\min}^p$, leading to a retail price below p_1, and lowering the EWS.

The above analysis has shown that within the range of equilibria a change in the level of aggregate demand leads to a change in the level of employment. It has not been necessary to specify the cause of the change in aggregate demand. The cause could be a nominal change such as an increase in the money supply. Since, within the equilibrium range, the retail price remained constant, a change in the nominal level of aggregate demand becomes a change in the real level of aggregate demand. It should be noted that the constancy of the retail price was not forced on the model but is an outcome that is consistent with the model. While the producer price rises with the aggregate level of output, the retail price can remain constant due to the customer market effect.

5.5 Calculating the Size of the Range of Equilibria

To calculate the size of the range of equilibria (the distance between n_2 and n_4 in figure 5.6) the constant-elasticity production function $q = b(en)^\beta$ is used. Along with the specific functional form assumed for the efficiency function, $e = v^\theta - \bar{v}^\phi$ with $0 < \theta$, $\phi < 1$, these assumptions yield, for the labour demand curve,

$$v = [(p^p/p)b\beta\theta^\beta n^{\beta-1}]^{1/(1-\beta\theta)} \tag{5.17}$$

The equation for the EWS is

$$v = [G^\phi(1-\theta)]^{1/(\theta-\phi)} \tag{5.18}$$

where G is defined by (5.9).

At a producer price of p^p_{min} the retail price is p_1. Normalize this retail price to unity. Then, from the labour demand curve (5.17) and the EWS (5.18), the level of employment determined by a producer price of p^p_{min} is the solution for n_{min} from

$$[p^p_{min} b\beta\theta^\beta (n_{min})^{\beta-1}]^{1/(1-\beta\theta)} = [(G_{min})^\phi/(1-\theta)]^{1/(\theta-\phi)} \qquad (5.19)$$

where G_{min} is the value of G when the aggregate employment ratio takes its minimum equilibrium value of zn_{min}/L.

With a producer price of p^p_{max} the retail price can again be equated to unity. The level of employment is then the solution for n_{max} from

$$[p^p_{max} b\beta\theta^\beta (n_{max})^{\beta-1}]^{1/(1-\beta\theta)} = [(G_{max})^\phi/(1-\theta)]^{1/(\theta-\phi)} \qquad (5.20)$$

where G_{max} is the value of G when the aggregate employment ratio takes its maximum equilibrium value of zn_{max}/L.

Dividing (5.19) by (5.20) and rearranging yields

$$n_{min}/n_{max} = [SG_{max}/G_{min}]^{\phi(1-\beta\theta)/(1-\beta)(\theta-\phi)} \qquad (5.21)$$

where $S = p^p_{min}/p^p_{max}$. From equation (5.21) a solution for the range of equilibrium levels of employment can be derived if either E_{max} or E_{min} is set exogenously.

Numerical values for the size of the equilibrium range of employment levels, defined as $(1 - n_{min}/n_{max}) \times 100$, based on (5.21), are reported in table 5.1. For all calculations E_{max} was set at 0.95, reflecting a minimum equilibrium rate of unemployment of 5 per cent. In addition, r was set at 0.1 and β at 0.75. From the discussion in chapter 4, a reasonable value of S lies between 0.9 and 0.99. Calculations based on three values, 0.9, 0.95 and 0.99, are reported. Three values of income if not working as a proportion of wages, s, are used, 0.25, 0.5 and 0.75: these cover reasonable values. There is little empirical knowledge about reasonable values for ϕ and θ. It was pointed out above that for the equilibrium level of the efficiency of labour to move pro-cyclically, ϕ has to be less than θ. However, it would seem unreasonable for the value of ϕ to differ markedly from the value of θ. Efficiency-wage

Table 5.1 *Ranges of equilibrium employment level (percentages);* $\beta=0.75$, $r = 0.1$, $E_{max} = 0.95$

| | | | | S | |
ϕ	θ	s	0.9	0.95	0.99
0.05	0.15	0.75	21.52	11.19	2.31
		0.5	15.21	7.86	1.61
		0.25	11.60	5.98	1.23
0.2	0.3	0.75	11.20	5.64	1.14
		0.5	6.53	3.27	0.65
		0.25	4.55	2.27	0.45
0.45	0.55	0.75	7.62	3.80	0.76
		0.5	4.19	2.08	0.41
		0.25	2.85	1.41	0.28
0.85	0.95	0.75	8.09	4.05	0.81
		0.5	4.48	2.23	0.46
		0.25	3.06	1.51	0.30

arguments are usually based on the value of wages *relative* to the opportunity cost of a job. For the cases reported in table 5.1, ϕ is assumed to be less than θ, but only by a small margin. One piece of empirical evidence on the size of ϕ and θ is in Krueger and Summers (1988). They combine estimates from Brown and Medoff (1978) and Dickens and Katz (1986) and postulate a value for θ of 0.03. These estimates are derived from calculations based on the turnover model of efficiency-wage theory. This, as was noted earlier, is only one of several types of models of efficiency-wage theory: therefore these estimates ignore the influence of high wages on efficiency that come from deterring shirking, attracting high-quality job applicants and raising morale. Krueger and Summers argue that, because only one of several bases for the efficiency-wage model was used, the value of 0.03 is probably an underestimate of the true value of θ. Calculations of the equilibrium range based on four pairs of values of ϕ and θ (0.05, 0.15; 0.2, 0.3; 0.45, 0.55; 0.85, 0.95) are reported. If one of the major efficiency-wage theories yields a θ of only 0.03 then probably the pair of smaller values of ϕ and θ in table 5.1 is the most realistic.

The entries in table 5.1 can be interpreted as follows. Take the top left-hand entry of 21.52. With $E_{max} = 0.95$, $\beta = 0.75$, $S = 0.9$, $\phi = 0.05$, $\theta = 0.15$ and $s = 0.75$, the minimum equilibrium rate of employment is 21.52 per cent less than the maximum equilibrium rate of employment. It is shown in table 5.1 that the higher unemployment benefits are, the larger is the range of equilibrium rates of employment.

It is also true that the size of the equilibrium range is increased if the elasticity of output with respect to labour input, β, or the difference between the effort-function parameters ϕ and θ, are raised. Reducing the rate of interest also can increase the size of the equilibrium range. These relationships between the size of the equilibrium range and the exogenous variables follow from (5.21).

5.6   Inflation and Unemployment

When transformed into the Phillips curve framework, a range of equilibrium levels of employment implies a range of equilibrium rates of unemployment. If unemployment is maintained at a rate within the equilibrium range then the rate of inflation will persist. Only if unemployment is forced outside the range will disequilibrium generate a persistent change in the rate of inflation.

Consider, for example, a monetary policy that maintains an aggregate level of employment such that at each firm the level of employment lies between n_{min} and n_{max}. Each firm will be choosing a wage payment such that the consumption real wage yields the optimal level of efficiency. The setting of retail prices will bring no pressure to alter the consumption real wage.

The equilibrium level of employment and the consumption real wage just described need not be disturbed in an inflationary environment. Suppose, for example, that retailers know that their customers expect retail prices to rise by x per cent. Then each retailer can raise his or her price by x per cent without dislodging any customers. Producers will raise money wages by x per cent to maintain the efficiency-optimizing value of the consumption real wage, and they will raise producer prices by x per cent in line with the x per cent rise in marginal cost. Provided that nominal aggregate demand is raised by x per cent, the economy remains at the initial equilibrium level of employment.

If the aggregate level of employment is outside the equilibrium range then there will be a state of disequilibrium. This will cause a change in prices. For example, assume that the government maintains an aggregate rate of employment corresponding to a level of employment at each firm which is less than n_{min}, such as the level n_1 shown in figure 5.6. At this aggregate level of employment and with a retail price of p_1, the consumption real wage which induces the optimal level of efficiency is w_1. At $\{w_1, n_1\}$ producers will wish to expand employment and will cut producer prices to expand sales. Retail prices will be reduced. Producers will then reduce money wages to re-establish the consumption real wage that optimizes the efficiency of workers. A deflationary spiral of prices will continue as long as employment is maintained below n_{min}. In terms of the long-run Phillips curve, maintaining the rate of unemployment in excess of the maximum equilibrium rate of unemployment will generate a falling rate of inflation.

The size of the equilibrium range of unemployment can be inferred from the calculations in table 5.1. For example, if $S = 0.95$, $r = 0.1$, $\beta = 0.75$, $\phi = 0.05$, $\theta = 0.15$, $s = 0.5$ and the minimum equilibrium rate of unemployment is 5 per cent, then the range of equilibrium unemployment levels is 7.47 percentage points (7.47 = 95 × 0.0786). To push unemployment below 5 per cent will accelerate the price level, but to decelerate the price level will require an unemployment rate in excess of 12.47 per cent.

Unfortunately, an evaluation of the importance of the customer market/efficiency-wage model which relies on the numerical calculations of table 5.1 is hampered by a lack of direct evidence on realistic values of ϕ and θ, the parameters of the effort function. It is not clear which pair of values of ϕ and θ in table 5.1 are closest to the truth. The numbers reported in table 5.1 show a significant decrease in the size of the range of equilibrium levels of employment as we move from $\{\phi = 0.05, \theta = 0.15\}$ to $\{\phi = 0.45, \theta = 0.55\}$. However, as ϕ and θ are raised further, the size of the range increases slightly. From this we can conclude from the model that a ratio of unemployment income to wages of 0.5 and a customer market step of 0.95 yield a range of equilibrium rates of unemployment of at least two percentage points. If the elasticity of effort with respect to wages is 0.2, then a range of equilibrium levels of unemployment of five percentage points or more would appear plausible.

5.7   Conclusion

The combination of retail price-setting, as suggested by the analysis of customer markets, and of wage-setting, as suggested by the theory of efficiency wages, has been shown in this chapter to be capable of generating a range of equilibrium rates of unemployment.

In the model economic agents optimize subject to the constraints that they face. Furthermore, within the equilibrium range, agents are not mistaken about the true values of relative prices. In equilibrium, behaviour is optimal and without error, and hence any rate of unemployment within the equilibrium range can persist without causing the rate of inflation to change. The disequilibrium processes which are the causes of change to the rate of inflation in the models of the long-run Phillips curve only operate when the rate of unemployment is forced outside the equilibrium range. By having a range of rates of unemployment consistent with a non-changing rate of inflation, the model may be thought of as Keynesian, and the combination of customer market price-setting and efficiency wages may be thought of as a microfoundation for Keynesian macroeconomics.

The model of this chapter will be hard to evaluate without quantitative knowledge of the relation between efficiency and real wages, because the equilibrium range is sensitive to the sizes of the parameters of the efficiency function. However, even without good estimates of the influence of wages on efficiency, the arguments of this chapter suggest that customer market theory, combined with efficiency-wage theory, yields a range of equilibrium rates of unemployment of at least two percentage points and possibly of five percentage points or more.

Part 4
Customer Markets, Group Wage Bargaining and the Range of Equilibria

6 Wage Bargaining and Specific Human Capital

When the marginal revenue product of employees exceeds the alternative wage, that is the wage from the next best employment opportunity, rents are earned. These rents have to be shared between the employer and the employee. In this chapter it is shown that by making a collective agreement with a firm to divide these rents, a pool of workers will prefer wages which can yield involuntary unemployment. The level of this involuntary unemployment is sensitive to the level of aggregate demand if retail prices are set in customer markets along the lines discussed in chapter 3. From this sensitivity of unemployment to aggregate demand a range of equilibrium levels of unemployment is derived.

An excess of the marginal revenue product of labour over the alternative wage can arise for several reasons. Costs of hiring and firing are an oft-cited source (see Nickell 1986, pp. 475–6, 517) for a review of the empirical knowledge on the size of hiring and firing costs). For some jobs, training can be undertaken which raises the worker's productivity at that job by more than at any other job. In virtually all jobs there is some specific knowledge to be accumulated, such as the layout of the workplace, the people to deal with over various matters arising during the course of work and the idiosyncracies of pieces of machinery. Furthermore, workers incur costs in searching and applying for a job. Following Becker (1962), the accumulation of these types of investment in employees is called specific human capital.

Hashimoto and Yu (1980) have analysed the division between the employer and an employee of rents earned on specific human capital. In their model the employer bargains with workers on an individual basis. To avoid strategic behaviour by either party, wages are set before the state of the world is revealed. If the formula agreed on for setting wages cannot allow adequately for all possible outcomes of labour demand, then involuntary unemployment can arise. Suppose, for example, that a rigid wage is set. If demand for labour turns out to be low, the employee will be laid off regardless of the relation between his or her marginal revenue product and the alternative wage. This involuntary unemployment results from ignorance of the level of labour demand at the time the wage is set. Under individual wage bargaining such unemployment may be short-lived. Once both parties agree that demand is low the incentive exists for renegotiating the wage downwards; employment will be restored provided that the marginal revenue product of labour exceeds the alternative wage.

In contrast to the temporary nature of involuntary unemployment that arises from the individual bargaining of the Hashimoto and Yu model, the model of McDonald and Solow (1981) shows that when workers as a group make wage agreements with a firm, then the wage desired by the group of workers can yield involuntary unemployment even when labour demand is known. It is assumed that both parties to the wage agreement know the level of labour demand when setting the wage, and that the wage can be reset whenever labour demand changes. In the McDonald and Solow model, ignorance of demand conditions need not be invoked to explain involuntary unemployment.

6.1 Collective Agreements on Wages and Employment

Consider a pool of labour of m people, each of whom has an accumulation of specific human capital sufficient to qualify for employment at a particular 'parent' firm. The total utility of this group is

$$W = nu(v) + (m - n)u(\bar{v}) \qquad (6.1)$$

where v is the real wage in terms of consumer purchasing power (= w/p), n is the employment of the labour pool at the parent firm and $\bar{v}$ is the real income receipts if laid off. Real income receipts if laid off includes unemployment benefits and the real income value of leisure.

Workers are assumed to act as a group in reacting to wages and employment offered by the firm: individual bargaining does not take place. It is assumed that the group is able to prevent anybody from undercutting the wage that optimizes the group's interest. Social pressure by members of the group on potential undercutters may be sufficient, or a trade union may be formed to help protect the wage desired by the group: indeed, as is shown below, the gains to labour from acting as a group are a stimulus to the formation of a trade union. A trade union organization can assist in preventing undercutting and can formulate wage demands which may help to keep wages closer to the group's optimum. Furthermore, a trade union can help to ensure that employment is maintained at its desired level.

Whether or not the group of workers forms a union, the analysis of this chapter assumes that the group has an open attitude to new members: that is, any number of new entrants are accepted into the pool and into the group's utility level, equation (6.1). A trade union dominated by a group of insiders who are unconcerned about the utility of new members is analysed in chapter 8.

Wages and employment are chosen to maximize the product of the net gain from employment by the group of workers (= $W - mu(\bar{v})$)) and the profits earned by the parent firm (= $R(n) - wn$); that is, to maximize

$$n[u(v) - u(\bar{v})][R(n) - wn] \qquad (6.2)$$

In (6.2) the general price level, p, which is independent of the actions of any single firm, is assumed to be equal to unity.

Maximizing (6.2) yields the Nash solution. The Nash solution can be derived from a set of four axioms (see, for example, de Menil (1971, pp. 8–14) for a discussion of the axioms that underlie the Nash solution). In the scenario being discussed here, members of the group are envisaged as being in agreement that these four axioms constitute fair practice in dividing up the rents from specific human capital. The Nash solution can be generalized by allowing for unequal weights on the pay-offs to the two parties. The choice of weights may be related to the split between employer and employee of the costs of accumulating the specific human capital. An optimal split of both costs and rents may arise from applying the arguments of Hashimoto and Yu (1980) to this model. That is not investigated here. As long as the weights are fixed, the equal-weight version of equation (5.2) is sufficient for the purposes of this chapter.

The first-order conditions for maximizing (6.2) by the choice of w and n may be written as

$$\{u(v) - u(\bar{v})\}/u'(v) = v - R'(n)/p, \tag{6.3}$$

$$v = \{R'(n) + R(n)/n\}/2p \tag{6.4}$$

As discussed in detail in McDonald and Solow (1981), equation (6.3) describes a contract curve of tangencies between indifference curves of a group of workers in the labour pool and isoprofit curves of a parent firm. The indifference curves are downward-sloping and asymptotic to $v = \bar{v}$. The isoprofit curves are hump-shaped, reaching their maximum where they cut the marginal revenue product of labour schedule. Sets of the indifference curves and the isoprofit curves are shown in figure 6.1. The contract curve is upward-sloping and cuts the marginal revenue product of labour curve at $\bar{v}$, at which point the contract curve is vertical. Outcomes along the contract curve describe tangencies between the indifference maps of the two parties. These outcomes are Pareto superior (for the two parties) to outcomes off the contract curve. Equation (6.4) is the arithmetic mean of the marginal and the average revenue products of labour. It is downward-sloping and is called the equity locus. The contract curve and the equity locus are shown in figure 6.1. Their intersection describes the Nash solution.

Shifts in the demand for the firm's product will shift both the contract curve and the equity locus horizontally in the same direction. An increase in demand shifts both curves to the right and a decrease shifts both curves to the left. As a result of this pattern, employment will move with demand.

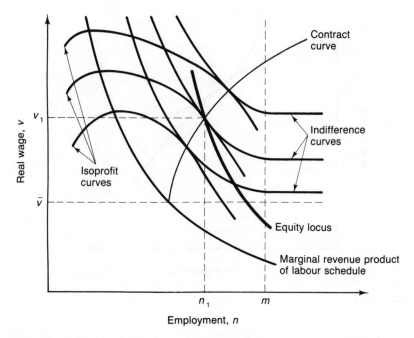

Figure 6.1

6.2 Group Wage Bargaining and Involuntary Unemployment

The agreement between the firm and its workers to share the rents from specific human capital yields a wage in excess of the opportunity cost of labour in the short run, $\bar{v}$. When demand is high and most or all of the labour pool is employed, there would be little downward pressure on this excess. Indeed, to attract new workers to the pool to replace those who leave, an excess of the wage over the short-run opportunity cost of labour will be necessary to compensate for any costs borne by the new workers in accumulating the specific human capital entailed in working at the firm. On the other hand, when demand is low the desire to attract additional members to the pool is weak or non-existent. The firm may wish to take advantage of a low level of demand by reducing wages. The sharing model predicts that workers will resist such downward pressure on wages, even though some of them would

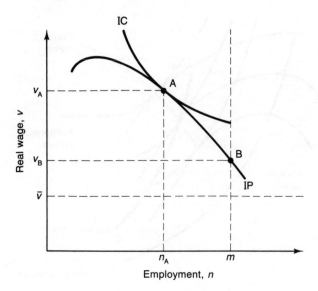

Figure 6.2

avoid involuntary unemployment if wages did decline. By contrast, with individual bargaining as in Hashimoto and Yu (1980), wages would be expected to fall when both parties recognize that demand is low, and this would eliminate involuntary unemployment.

To see why the sharing of rents from specific human capital between the firm and a group of workers leads to involuntary unemployment, consider figure 6.2. In figure 6.2 $\{v_A, n_A\}$ are the wage and employment outcomes that satisfy the conditions for the Nash solution. Assume that demand is low and that the size of the labour pool, m, exceeds n_A. In figure 6.2, IC is the indifference curve of the group of workers: it represents a particular level of group utility. The isoprofit curve of the firm, IP, shows the level of profits attained. The curves intersect at A. If wages were reduced to v_B, employment could be expanded to m with no reduction in the firm's profits. This is point B in figure 6.2. At point B, with employment equal to m, no one in the pool of workers is unemployed. However, the group of workers prefers point A to B because the group's utility is higher at A than B. Therefore the group prefers the existence of involuntary unemployment. Moving down the isoprofit curve from A, the gain to the utility of the group due to higher levels of employment is more than offset by the loss to the utility of the group due to lower wages. Of course, those individuals lucky enough to switch from unemployment to employment gain. However, from the group's point of view their gain is more than offset by the loss from lower wages.

This explanation of why the maximization of the group's objective leads to involuntary unemployment applies not only to the analysis of this chapter but also to the analysis of trades unions in chapter 7.

6.3 The Range of Macroeconomic Equilibria

To develop a macroeconomic model combining collective labour agreements with retailing in customer markets assume, along the lines of the efficiency-wagecustomer market model of chapter 5, that producers sell to retailers who sell in customer markets. Assume z producers, each setting wages and employment for its pool of labour according to the Nash solution and each selling output to the many shops which retail in customer markets. Lay-off pay is simply unemployment benefits, fixed in real terms, and the value of leisure if not working. In keeping with the idea that the agreements with the labour pool are short term, earnings from subsequent employment opportunities for laid-off workers are not included in lay-off pay. Laid-off workers who gain employment with another producer are deemed to have left the original labour pool, and so those earnings do not appear as a receipt of a pool member.

Assume, for simplicity, that competition between producers forces the producer price down to marginal cost. With competition, the revenue function of a producer is $p^p f(n)$, where $f(n)$ is the production function. Substituting this revenue function into (6.3) and (6.4) and combining the resulting equations yields

$$\varepsilon = (1 + \beta) / (1 - \beta) \tag{6.5}$$

where $\varepsilon = v u'(v) / (u(v) - u(\bar{v}))$ is the elasticity of the gain from employment with respect to the wage and β is the elasticity of output with respect to employment ($\beta = nf'(n)/f(n)$). With perfect competition between producers, the level of demand is reflected in the size of the producer price. But the producer price does not enter (6.5). Consequently, changes in demand and thus in producer price do not change the bargained real wage. However, changes in producer price *do* affect the level of employment. With revenue given by $p^p f(n)$, the equity locus (6.4) becomes

$$v = \frac{p^p}{p}\left[\frac{f'(n) + f(n)/n}{2}\right] \tag{6.6}$$

According to (6.6) a rise in the ratio of producer price to retail price will raise the level of employment. To see this differentiate (6.6) to obtain (after substituting (6.6) back into the derivative)

$$\frac{dn}{d(p^p/p)} = \frac{-2wn}{(p^p/p)\{p^p f''(n)n + 2[w - p^p f(n)/n]\}} \tag{6.7}$$

A positive level of profits implies that the term $[w - p^p f(n)/n]$ is negative and thus $dn/d(p^p/p)$ is positive.

The determination of employment for one of the producers is shown in figure 6.3. The horizontal schedule is (6.5), which determines the bargained wage independently of the price ratio p^p/p. The downward-sloping schedule is the equity locus (6.6). The intersection of these schedules at $n = n_1$ determines the equilibrium level of employment. An increase in the price ratio p^p/p will shift the downward-sloping equity locus to the right (as shown by the positive sign of the derivative (6.7)) and increase employment.

As shown in chapter 3, if retailers sell in customer markets then the price ratio p^p/p has a range of values consistent with profit-maximizing equilibrium. Applying this range to figure 6.3 implies a range of equilibrium levels of employment at a particular producer. With z identical producers, and assuming that retailers can operate without labour, the aggregate level of employment in this simple macroeconomy is zn. Thus there is a range of equilibrium levels of aggregate employment.

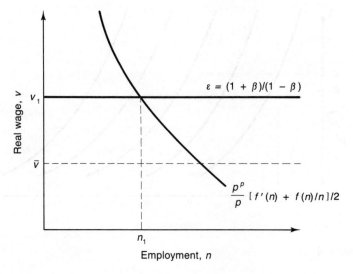

Figure 6.3

6.4 Aggregate Demand and Employment

Shifts in the level of aggregate demand will shift the demand curve facing individual retailers. In figure 6.4 are shown five locations of this demand curve for a representative retailer, reflecting five levels of aggregate demand. In figure 6.5 five contract curves and five equity locii are shown. These contract curves and equity locii reflect five values of the producer price. They are drawn assuming a particular value for the retail price. The vertical axis is money wages. A change in retail price will shift the contract curves.

For each of the five values of the producer price there is a contract curve and an equity locus. The higher the producer price the further to the right are the contract curve and the equity locus and so the greater is the level of employment and output. These five values of producer price are selected so that aggregate output is equal to aggregate retail sales. For example, consider the contract curve CC_3 and the equity locus EL_3. The producer price on which CC_3 and EL_3 are based is labelled p_3^p. At this producer price

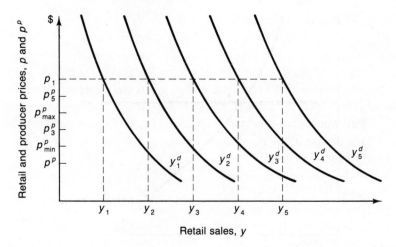

Figure 6.4

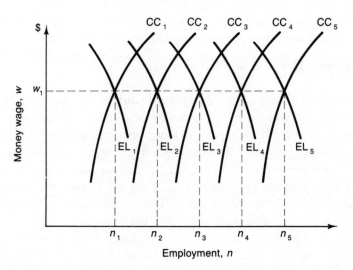

Figure 6.5

the aggregate output is zq_3, the output of each producer times the number of producers, z. In figure 6.4, at the demand curve y_3^d the typical retailer sells y_3 units of the good at a retail price of p_1. Aggregate retail sales are equal to y_3 times the number of retailers.

Assume that this aggregate is equal to zq_3. If p_3^p lies in the interval of p_{min}^p to p_{max}^p, then the configuration of retail demand curve y_3^d, contract curve CC_3 and equity locus EL_3 yields a macroeconomic equilibrium. With this configuration and a producer price of p_3^p, the profit-maximizing retail price is p_1. A retail price of p_1 and a producer price of p_3^p induces an aggregate level of employment of zn_3 and an aggregate level of output of zq_3. The latter satisfies the aggregate demand for goods.

The configurations of $\{y_2^d, CC_2, EL_2\}$ and $\{y_4^d, CC_4, EL_4\}$ shown in figures 6.4 and 6.5 are consistent with macroeconomic equilibrium. With $\{y_2^d, CC_2, EL_2\}$ a producer price equal to p_{min}^p induces aggregate employment of zn_2 and aggregate output of zq_2. The latter is equal to the level of aggregate retail sales when each retailer faces a demand curve of y_2^d and sets a retail price of p_1. A producer price of p_{min}^p is the minimum producer price consistent with a profit-maximizing retail price of p_1. At the configuration $\{y_4^d, CC_4, EL_4\}$ the producer price of p_{max}^p is the maximum producer price consistent with a profit-maximizing retail price of p_1.

With the configurations of the retail demand curve, contract curve and equity locus $\{y_1^d, CC_1, EL_1\}$ and $\{y_5^d, CC_5, EL_5\}$ there is no macroeconomic equilibrium. At $\{y_1^d, CC_1, EL_1\}$, a producer price of p_1^p that equates aggregate supply with aggregate retail sales of y_1 times the number of retailers is below p_{min}^p. A producer price below p_{min}^p will cause retailers to reduce the retail price below p_1, shifting the contract curve and equity locus and upsetting the configuration $\{y_1^d, CC_1, EL_1\}$. On the other hand, at $\{y_5^d, CC_5, EL_5\}$ a producer price of p_5^p, which is greater than p_{max}^p, is required to generate enough production to satisfy aggregate demand. A producer price about p_{max}^p will, however, lead to an increase in retail price and upset the configuration $\{y_5^d, CC_5, EL_5\}$.

6.5 Calculating the Size of the Range of Equilibria

To calculate the size of the range of equilibria (the distance between n_2 and n_4 in figure 6.5) the constant-elasticity production function, $q = bn^\beta$, with $0 < \beta < 1$, and the constant-elasticity utility function, $u = w^\gamma / \gamma$ with $\gamma \leq 1$, are used. With these functional forms the general equations for the contract curve and the equity locus are

$$v\left[1 - \frac{1 - (\bar{v}/v)^\gamma}{\gamma}\right] = p^p b \beta n^{\beta-1}/p, \qquad (6.3')$$

$$v = p^p b n^{\beta-1}(1+\beta)/2p \qquad (6.4')$$

From (6.3') and (6.4') an expression determining n can be obtained. That expression is

$$n = [p^p b(1+\beta)/2k\bar{v}]^{1/(1-\beta)} \qquad (6.8)$$

Setting $p^p = p^p_{min}$ in (6.8) determines the minimum equilibrium level of employment, n_{min}. (In figure 6.5, n_2 is the n_{min} level.) Setting $p^p = p^p_{max}$ in (6.8) determines the maximum equilibrium level of employment, n_{max} (which is n_4 in figure 6.5). Taking the ratio of n_{min} to n_{max}, the range of equilibrium levels of employment is

$$n_{min}/n_{max} = S^{1/(1-\beta)} \qquad (6.9)$$

where $S = p^p_{min}/p^p_{max}$.

Equation (6.9), which determines the size of the range of equilibrium levels of employment, is extremely simple: it has only two parameters, the price ratio, S, and the elasticity of output with respect to labour input, β. In table 6.1 calculations of the range expressed as $(1 - n_{min}/n_{max}) \times 100$ for three values of S (0.90, 0.95 and 0.99), and three values of β (0.5, 0.75 and 0.95), are given. The impact of increasing β is large. As β approaches 1, the equilibrium range approaches 100 per cent. As table 6.1 shows, the ranges of equilibria are, in general, quite large.

Comparing the group wage-setting model with the efficiency-wage model of chapter 5, it appears that group wage-setting yields larger ranges of equilibria. For example, with $S = 0.95$ and $\beta = 0.75$, the group wage-setting model yields a range of equilibria of 18.55 per cent. In the efficiency-wage model with these values of S and β, the largest size of the range recorded in table 5.1 is 11.19, which occurs when $\phi = 0.05$ and $\theta = 0.15$. One factor which helps to explain why the range is large in the group wage-setting model is the different treatment of real income receipts if laid off. With

Table 6.1 Ranges of equilibrium employment level (percentages)

	S		
	0.9	0.95	0.99
β			
0.5	19.00	9.75	1.99
0.75	34.39	18.55	3.94
0.95	77.84	64.15	18.21

group wage-setting, real income receipts if laid off are determined only by unemployment benefits and the value of leisure. Receipts from alternative jobs are excluded because a worker who takes an alternative job is assumed to have left the group. For the efficiency-wage model, decision-making is by individuals and hence takes into account future employment opportunities. Because of this difference, in the group wage-setting model $\bar{v}$ is a constant, while in the efficiency-wage model $\bar{v}$ is positively related to the aggregate level of employment. This positive relationship is embodied in the efficiency-wage schedule. The steeper the efficiency-wage schedule is, the smaller is the range of equilibrium levels of employment.

The next two chapters analyse different models of group wage-setting. In those models unions take a more aggressive role in wage determination. However, it will be seen that in all the group wage-setting models the equation determining the size of the range of equilibria is the same as equation (6.9).

7 Wage-setting by
an Open Trade Union

In chapter 6 rents were considered to arise from specific human capital embodied in workers. These rents were divided between workers and the firm. To ensure fair play by the firm in the division of the rents from specific human capital, workers may form a trade union. However, trades unions may have more ambitious aims. In particular, monopoly rents earned by the firm from exercising market power in selling its output may become a target which more aggressive trade unions attempt to appropriate. In this chapter and the next, the implications for wages and employment of these more aggressive trade unions are considered.

The trade union analysed in this chapter is assumed to have an 'open-door' policy to new members; that is, the interests of new members are given an equal weight with those of existing members. As a result the objective function of the union trades wages for employment. The idea that the objective of a union incorporates a trade-off between wages and employment is the natural assumption for economists to make. The plausibility of this assumption is discussed below. However, some economists, especially Lindbeck and Snower (1984), Blanchard and Summers (1986) and Carruth and Oswald (1987), argue that trade unions are dominated by their employed members. These workers are often called insiders. The insiders do not gain from an expansion in employment and so are not willing to trade off wages for employment. A union of this type, called an insider-dominated union, is analysed in chapter 8.

The open trade union of this chapter is assumed to set the wage unilaterally, but to have no control over employment: employment is controlled by the firm. This wage-setting union has been called the 'simple monopoly union' (see McDonald and Solow, 1981, p. 897). With a simple monopoly union the wage and employment outcomes are on the labour demand curve. As is well known, these outcomes are inefficient. Efficient outcomes, from which both the union and the firm can benefit, are on a contract curve. However, in this chapter efficient bargains are eschewed: efficient bargains were analysed in the previous chapter. While that chapter was concerned with the division of rents from specific human capital between workers and the firm, that analysis could be carried over virtually unchanged to the case of an open trade union appropriating a firm's monopoly rents. The only change would be to reinterpret the rents more broadly. So in the interests of completeness, this chapter analyses the simple monopoly union.

Although efficient bargains are Pareto optimal outcomes for the two bargaining parties, simple monopoly outcomes may still dominate in practice. Starting from an efficient bargain, the employer, by keeping the wage unchanged but reducing employment, can raise profits. If the bargain divides rents from specific human capital, as in the previous chapter, the employer may have little incentive to reduce employment in this way, because the rents distributed to labour, being a return on outlays made by labour to accumulate specific human capital, attract labour to the employer's labour pool. However, with an aggressive trade union, remuneration for unionized workers may be significantly above the amount necessary to attract labour to the pool. With high wages the employer will be less concerned about the adverse impact on the recruitment of workers of moving away from efficient bargains because with high wages there will be no shortage of recruits.

The empirical importance of simple monopoly bargains relative to efficient bargains is not settled. The number of unions that can achieve efficient bargains is not known. Empirical investigations (see Brown and Ashenfelter, 1986; Eberts and Stone, 1986; Mac-Curdy and Pencavel, 1986) have found some evidence favouring the existence of efficient bargains, but that evidence is weak.

7.1 Wage Demands by a Simple Monopoly Trade Union

Assume that the union acts as a simple monopolist setting the money wage (w) unilaterally and allowing the employer discretion over employment (n). The union has m members, all with identical utility functions. Assuming that n of the members are selected randomly for employment, a democratic union will vote for wage settlements that maximize the expected utility of each of the m identical members. Each member has a probability n/m of having a job and achieving a level of utility $u(w/p)$, where p is the general level of retail prices. Alternatively, the union member is unemployed with probability $(1 - n/m)$, and achieves a level of utility $u(\bar{v})$, where $\bar{v}$ is the real value of unemployment benefits plus the real income value of leisure. With these alternatives, the expected utility of the union member is

$$(n/m)u(w/p) + (1 - n/m)u(\bar{v}) \tag{7.1}$$

A random employment rule which gives all members of the union, whether employed or not, an equal chance of employment has been observed, although rarely: an example is to be found in the London docks in the nineteenth century. However, (7.1) also describes a union contemplating a downswing in demand in which workers laid-off will be selected at random. In that situation the initial level of employment can be identified with m in (7.1). In evaluating the wage and employment outcomes following a decline in demand, the m employed workers will trade wages for employment according to objective (7.1).

Instead of treating the union's objective as the expected utility of a representative member, an alternative is to define the union's objective as the collective welfare, W, where W is the summation of the utility of the employed members and the unemployed members; that is,

$$W = nu(w/p) + (m - n)u(\bar{v}) \tag{7.2}$$

Objective (7.2) applies to a union which takes into account the interests of all its members. While democratic procedures may suggest that unions become dominated by a subgroup of members (the case to be analysed in chapter 8), the history of the trade union movement emphasizes the importance of concepts such as the 'brotherhood of man', and the solidarity of the working class and has espoused slogans such as 'Workers of the World, Unite!'. These sentiments argue against the idea that unions are dominated by a selfish subgroup of members and suggest a broader constituency of interest, such as that reflected in (7.2).

Assuming that the number of members is outside the union's control, the two objectives (7.1) and (7.2) are equivalent. Multiplying (7.1) by m yields (7.2). Both cases can be summarized by assuming that the union wishes to maximize

$$n\{u(w/p) - u(\bar{v})\} + mu(\bar{v}) \tag{7.3}$$

Objective (7.3) can be represented in wages–employment space by a map of downward-sloping indifference curves, which are asymptotic to a real wage equal to $\bar{v}$. For employment greater than the union's membership, the indifference curves are horizontal. Thus the indifference curves kink at $n = m$: a map is shown in figure 7.1. For levels of employment less than m, the union is prepared to trade wages for employment.

In response to the wage set by the union, the firm sets the level of employment to maximize profits. This will be the level of employment at which the marginal revenue product of labour is equal to the wage rate. Writing $R(n)$ as the firm's concave revenue function, the employment rule is to set employment on the labour demand curve, $w = R'(n)$. In setting the wage the union takes into account the employment response of the firm. Thus the union chooses the wage which maximizes its objective, subject to the condition that the level of employment will be on the labour demand curve. In figure 7.1 a wage demand of w^*/p is the optimal choice for the union. At this wage the labour demand curve is tangential to the union indifference curve. The first-order condition for this optimum can be written as

$$\varepsilon = E_{nw} \tag{7.4}$$

where $\varepsilon = vu'(v)/\{u(v) - u(\bar{v})\}$ is the elasticity of the gain from employment with respect to the real wage and $E_{nw} = -w/nR''(n)$ is the elasticity of the demand for labour with respect to the money wage, taken positively. Because the individual union and the

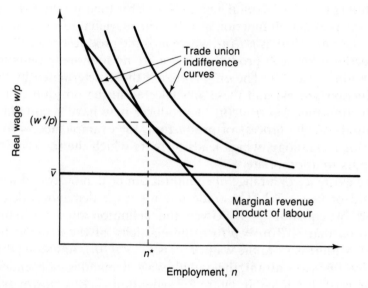

Figure 7.1

individual firm act as though they have no effect on the general level of retail prices, elasticities with respect to real and money wages can both appear in (7.4). Condition (7.4) ties the union's desired wage to $\bar{v}$ via the elasticity of the marginal revenue product of labour function and the form of the trade union members' utility function.

7.2 The Range of Macroequilibria

To construct a macroeconomic model from which a range of equilibrium levels of employment will be derived, assume that there are z producers in the economy, each with an identical production function and each facing a unionized labour pool. Each union operates on the lines explained in section 7.1. The producers sell to retailers who sell in customer markets. Retailers employ no labour.

For simplicity, assume that competition between producers forces the producer price down to the marginal cost of production.

Producers face a horizontal demand curve for their product. Then, with the production function $q = f(n)$, the marginal revenue product of labour, $R'(n)$, is $p^p f'(n)$, where p^p is the producer price. With competition between producers, there are no monopoly rents for the union to extract. The only rents are those determined by the production process and these are reflected in the position of the production function $q = f(n)$. A producer may have a particular advantage in the process of production, for example access to a superior technology, which leads to rents which the trade union attempts to appropriate.

The existence of a range of equilibria can be demonstrated with the aid of figure 7.2. The trade union's wage demand is determined by equation (7.4). Given the definition of the revenue function, that is $R(n) = p^p f(n)$, the elasticity of the demand for labour with respect to the wage, E_{nw}, is $f'(n)/nf''(n)$. Assuming that $f'(n)/nf''(n)$ is a constant, the union's wage demand is independent of the producer price. In figure 7.2, equation (7.4) is shown as a horizontal line, reflecting the assumed constancy of E_{nw}. The level of employment is determined by the condition that the money wage rate equals the marginal revenue product of labour, namely $w = p^p f'(n)$. Deflating both sides by the level of retail prices, the equation determining employment can be written as

$$v = \frac{p^p}{p} f'(n) \tag{7.5}$$

Equation (7.5) is represented by the downward-sloping curve in figure 7.2. The equilibrium level of employment is determined at the intersection of the two curves in figure 7.2; that is, at $n = n_1$.

In figure 7.2 an increase in the price ratio, p^p/p, will shift the labour demand curve to the right and increase the equilibrium level of employment. Because retailers are assumed to sell in customer markets, there is a range of equilibrium values of the price ratio p^p/p. This implies a range of equilibrium values of employment for the producer. Because of the assumption of a fixed number of identical producers, z, who account for all the employment in the economy, the aggregate level of employment is zn. Given the range of equilibrium values of p^p/p there is, then, a range of equilibrium levels of aggregate employment.

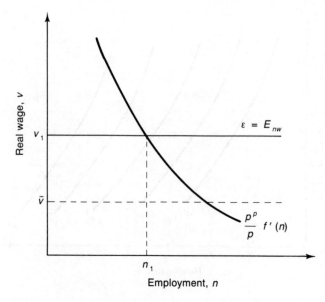

Figure 7.2

7.3   Aggregate Demand and Employment

This section shows how the level of aggregate demand determines where the economy will settle within the range of equilibrium levels of employment. In figure 7.3 five demand curves facing a representative retailer are shown. The curves reflect five levels of aggregate demand. At a retail price of p_1 the levels of retail sales corresponding to each level of demand are shown as y_1, y_2, y_3, y_4 and y_5. At these levels of retail sales lies the vertical section in the marginal revenue curve corresponding to that demand curve. These vertical sections are each bounded by p^p_{max} and p^p_{min}, shown on the vertical axis.

A producer price of p^p_{min} yields a demand curve to the representative producer of $p^p_{min} f'(n)$ shown in figure 7.4. The five trade

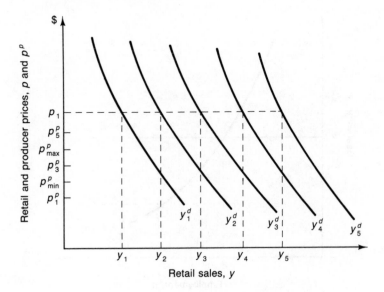

Figure 7.3

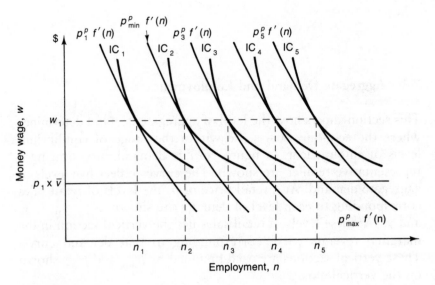

Figure 7.4

union indifference curves shown in figure 7.4, ic_1 to ic_5, are drawn on the assumption that the general level of retail prices equals p_1. (In figure 7.4 the vertical axis is measured in nominal wages. A change in the general level of retail prices would therefore shift the trade union indifference curves shown in the figure.) With a producer price of p^p_{min}, the union sets a wage of w_1 and the producer offers employment of n_2. Assuming that the aggregate level of production $(= zq_2 = zf(n_2))$ is equal to the aggregate level of retail sales $(= y_2$ times the number of retailers), the configuration $\{p_1, y_2, p^p_{min}, w_1, n_2\}$ is a macroeconomic equilibrium.

A level of aggregate demand yielding a demand curve y^d_3 facing the representative retailer can also yield a macroeconomic equilibrium. With y^d_3, a retail price of p_1 induces retail sales of y_3. Aggregate retail sales are y_3 times the number of retailers. For an equivalent aggregate level of output $(= zq_3)$ to be produced, a producer price of p^p_3 is necessary. With a producer price of p^p_3 the producer's demand curve for labour is $p^p_3 f'(n)$. The trade union's wage demand will be w_1 and the level of employment offered by a producer will be n_3. n_3 workers produce the level of output, q_3, required to satisfy aggregate demand. Because p^p_3 lies between p^p_{min} and p^p_{max}, the profit-maximizing retail price of retailers will be p_1. We can see, therefore, that $\{p_1, y_3, p^p_3, w_1, n_3\}$ describes a macroeconomic equilibrium.

The highest level of employment consistent with macroeconomic equilibrium is n_4. A level of aggregate demand leading to a demand curve facing the representative retailer of y^d_4 can induce $\{p_1, y_4, p^p_{max}, w_1, n_4\}$. However, higher levels of aggregate demand, such as the level leading to a demand curve facing the representative retailer of y^d_5, will not induce equilibrium levels of employment. A retail demand curve of y^d_5 would require a producer price of p^p_5 to induce a level of production sufficient to satisfy aggregate demand. A producer price of p^p_5 exceeds p^p_{max} and so will cause retailers to raise the retail price. The change in retail price will shift the indifference curves in figure 7.4 and will generate an increase in the trade union's wage demand. There can be no macroeconomic equilibrium at a level of employment of n_5.

Levels of employment below n_2 are not consistent with macroeconomic equilibrium. The range of macroeconomic equilibrium levels of employment runs from n_2 to n_4.

7.4 Calculating the Size of the Range of Equilibria

To calculate the size of the range of equilibria, constant-elasticity expressions are used for the firm's production function and demand function. The firm's output, q, is related to labour input by $q = bn^\beta$, where $0 < \beta < 1$ and $b > 0$, and the producer price p^p is related to the firm's output by $p^p = aq^{\alpha-1}$, where $\alpha < 1$ and $a > 0$. With these constant-elasticity specifications, the producer's marginal revenue product of labour is $R'(n) = \alpha\beta b^\alpha a n^{\alpha\beta-1}$, which makes $E_{nw} = (1 - \beta)^{-1}$. The constant-elasticity utility function, $u = (w/p)^\gamma/\gamma$, where $\gamma \leqslant 1$ will also be used. With these functional forms a union's optimal wage demand, given by equation (7.4), becomes

$$w/p = \{1 + \gamma(\alpha\beta - 1)\}^{-1/\gamma}\, \bar{v} = k\bar{v} \tag{7.6}$$

To calculate the size of the range of equilibria (the distance between n_2 and n_4 in figure 7.4), consider the producer's labour demand curve. Assuming $\alpha = 1$, when $p^p = p^p_{\min}$, the producer's labour demand curve is $w = p^p_{\min} b\beta n^{\beta-1}$, and n_2 is determined by

$$w_1 = p^p_{\min} b\beta n_2^{\beta-1} \tag{7.7}$$

When $p^p = p^p_{\max}$ the equilibrium level of employment is n_4. This level is determined by

$$w_1 = p^p_{\max} b\beta n_4^{\beta-1} \tag{7.8}$$

From (7.7) and (7.8) the range of equilibrium levels of employment is

$$n_{\min}/n_{\max} = S^{1/(1-\beta)} \tag{7.9}$$

where n_2 has been written as $n_{\min}$, n_4 has been written as $n_{\max}$ and $S = p^p_{\min}/p^p_{\max}$.

Now allow for a downward-sloping demand curve facing the producer. In this case the producer can set producer price to exploit some market power in selling to retailers. The demand curve facing a producer is $p^p = aq^{\alpha-1}$. Continue to assume that producers are identical. The level of aggregate demand that induces a retailer's demand curve of y_1^d is assumed to induce a profit-maximizing producer price of $p_{\min}^p$ at an employment level of n_2. The shift parameter, a, in the producer's demand curve is labelled a_2 for this level of aggregate demand. Thus $p_{\min}^p = a_2 q_2^{\alpha-1}$. Using the production function to substitute for q_2, a_2 is given by

$$a_2 = p_{\min}^p b^{1-\alpha} n_2^{\beta(1-\alpha)} \qquad (7.10)$$

Substituting this into the labour demand curve, $w = ab^\alpha \alpha \beta n^{\alpha\beta-1}$, the level of employment n_2 is determined by

$$w_1 = b\alpha\beta p_{\min}^p n_2^{\beta-1} \qquad (7.11)$$

By a similar argument, n_4 is determined by

$$w_1 = b\alpha\beta p_{\max}^p n_4^{\beta-1} \qquad (7.12)$$

From (7.11) and (7.12) the range of equilibrium levels of employment can be derived: it turns out to be the same as equation (7.9). Thus the existence of a downward-sloping demand curve facing producers does not affect the size of the range of macroeconomic equilibria.

The equation describing the equilibrium range for an economy in which trades unions set wages according to the simple monopoly union model is identical to the equation for the equilibrium range derived in the previous chapter, where wages and employment were set to share rents accruing from specific human capital. Moving from a loosely organized pool of labour to a more aggressive trade union has not affected the size of the equilibrium range. Only the vertical size of the discontinuity in the retailer's marginal revenue curve and the elasticity of the output of producers with respect to their labour input influence the size of the equilibrium range. The values in table 6.1 given in the previous chapter carry over to the case of the simple monopoly union.

8 Wage-bargaining with an Insider-dominated Trade Union

In chapter 7 it was shown that involuntary unemployment can arise when a group of workers form a trade union to make and enforce wage agreements. In the analysis the union was assumed to act in the interests of both employed and unemployed members. As a consequence of this assumption, the objective function of the union traded wages for employment. In this chapter a different type of union is modelled. It is assumed that the union is dominated by a subgroup of insiders who enjoy a high degree of job security. The objective function of this union does not incorporate a trade-off between wages and employment: the union's objective is simply to maximize the wage. In spite of this apparently very different assumption about the union's objective, the wage-setting practices turn out to be similar to those of the union which is prepared to trade wages for employment. Furthermore, for the two types of union the equations determining the size of the range of equilibria are the same.

A number of authors have given considerable emphasis to the idea that the union's objective is based on the utility of employed 'insiders'. McDonald and Solow (1980, 1984), Chapman and Fisher (1984), Borland (1985), Lindbeck and Snower (1985), Solow (1985), Oswald (1985), Blanchard and Summers (1986), Carruth and Oswald (1987), and McDonald (1989b) are among those who emphasize the contrast between insiders and outsiders. The nomenclature, 'insiders' and 'outsiders' is due to Lindbeck and Snower. The authors of these papers argue that insiders dominate the trade union's decision-making processes and that these insiders do not take into account the interests of the unemployed. If the group of insiders that dominates the union corresponds to those in employment, then, as discussed in McDonald and Solow (1984), there is a travelling kink in the union's indifference curves. The kink is located at the current level of employment and its position changes when employment changes. The travelling kink leads to somewhat irregular patterns of wage behaviour. Changes in the demand for labour can, in some circumstances, change wages but not employment and, in other circumstances, change employment but not wages. The fact that, in practice, a pattern of changes in wages and no changes in employment is not observed casts doubt on the empirical relevance of the trade union models with a travelling kink.

In this chapter a model of trade union behaviour is developed which rests on the realistic assumption that insiders dominate the trade union, but which does not lead to unrealistic patterns of wage and employment behaviour. The problems of the travelling kink models are avoided in this model. Here it is assumed that the union is dominated by a subgroup of the employed, and that members of this subgroup enjoy secure employment. Furthermore, it is assumed that the bargain over wages and employment is the result of a power struggle between the union and the firm. The behaviour of the bargained wage, that is its response to the exogeneous variables, is essentially the same as the wage behaviour in the models of McDonald and Solow (1981). The irregularities exhibited by other models with insider-dominance are avoided.

8.1   Wage Bargaining and the Insider-dominated Union

Union decision-making on wage negotiations is usually subject to some form of democratic control. Even if there is no direct voting on wage negotiations, the union officials responsible for negotiating with the employer are typically elected, and face defeat if a significant group of members judge their performance unfavourably. It is not clear how large a group has to be to dominate. The

51 per cent figure of the median voter model appears to be both too large and too small. One frequently hears complaints of low attendance and participation in important union meetings and elections, suggesting that 51 per cent is too large. On the other hand, for 51 per cent of members to attempt a wage demand that would lead to the lay-off of the other 49 per cent would be courting danger. To prevent a large disgruntled group from under-cutting wages would be very difficult. In any event, it seems reasonable to argue that the union will act in the interests of less than 100 per cent of its employed members.

Lay-off by seniority is a common practice. In the USA, first in – last out is often specified in labour contracts. In other industrial-ized countries seniority provisions appear to be important (see Oswald, unpublished). With lay-off by seniority, the jobs of the insiders who dominate the union will not be at risk for most fluctuations in employment. A very large decline in employment of, say, 10 per cent leaves 90 per cent of insiders employed. Since the dominating group usually has no need to worry about job security, its objective will be simply to maximize the wage. There-fore the union's objective is simply $u(w/p)$, where $u(\ )$ is the concave utility function of a representative member of the domi-nating group, w is the money wage and p is the level of retail prices.

In negotiating over wages and employment, the dominating group faces the risk that negotiations may break down and em-ployment will collapse to zero. A strike could lead to such an outcome, or the firm may cease operations due to bankruptcy. In bargaining, the reservation or no-contract outcome is $u(\bar{v})$, where $\bar{v}$ is income if laid off. In the short run, $\bar{v}$ would be mainly composed of the real value of unemployment benefits and the real income value of leisure if laid off.

From these considerations, the union regards its pay-off from bargaining as $[u(w/p) - u(\bar{v})]$. The firm is interested in profits, $\Pi = R(n) - wn$, where $R(n)$ is the concave revenue function and n is the level of employment. The fall-back level of profits, the level if operations cease, is assumed to be zero. Defining $\phi \in \{0, 1\}$ as the relative power of the union in bargaining, the outcome of the bargaining process is the levels of w and n which maximize

$$[u(w/p) - u(\bar{v})]^{\phi}[R(n) - wn]^{1-\phi} \tag{8.1}$$

The model emphasizes the degree of union power relative to that of the employer. This concept of union power is the ability to divide up the economic rents from employment to the union's advantage. Skill in wage negotiations would be one determinant of this power. The charisma of union leaders, that is their ability to hold members together and keep up the support of members during wage negotiations, is another.

There are some factors which, in general discussions, are included in union power but which enter this model through parameters other than that of power. For example, commentators sometimes assert that union power increases as the aggregate level of unemployment declines. However, if this assertion is based on the idea that alternative employment prospects increase in the upswing of the business cycle then the parameter in the model that measures lay-off pay, that is $\bar{v}$, would include this aspect of union power. If the cost of disagreement to the firm rises in an upswing this would be captured in the definition of the fall-back level of profits. A low value of the elasticity of labour demand captures the 'power' of a union, which arises from the fact that its members produce a product which has poor substitutes.

The first-order conditions for the problem of maximizing (8.1) by choice of w and n are:

$$w = R'(n), \tag{8.2}$$

$$\frac{vu'(v)}{u(v) - u(\bar{v})} = \left[\Phi\left(\frac{R(n)}{wn}\right) - 1 \right]^{-1} \tag{8.3}$$

where $v = w/p$ is the real wage and $\Phi = \phi/(1 - \phi)$. From (8.2) the equilibrium levels of the wage and the level of employment lie on the marginal revenue product of the labour schedule. As Oswald (unpublished) has shown, for a union which places no value on the level of employment, efficient bargains lie on the labour demand curve. By substitution of (8.2), (8.3) can be written as

$$\varepsilon = \beta / \Phi(1 - \beta) \tag{8.4}$$

where $\varepsilon = vu'(v)/[u(v) - u(\bar{v})]$ is the elasticity of the gain from employment with respect to the real wage and $\beta = R'(n)n/R(n)$ is the elasticity of revenue with respect to employment. From (8.4) it can be seen that a shift in the demand for labour that leaves the elasticity of the revenue function, β, unchanged will also leave the wage unchanged. Employment would bear the brunt of the adjustment to changes in demand. If changes in demand changed the value of β then the equilibrium wage would change. For example, if the revenue function is a cubic equation containing a region of increasing returns to labour, then, as shown in McDonald (1989a), positive shifts in demand will reduce the elasticity of revenue with respect to employment at any particular wage rate and this will, by (8.4), lead to a rise in the equilibrium wage. In this case increases in demand would lead to increases in wages as well as in employment. Another possibility is that the value of β at a particular wage will increase following a positive shift in demand. If markets become more competitive as they become larger, a proposition argued by Rotemberg and Salomer (1986), then β would respond in this way. With this pattern the equilibrium wage would fall as demand rose. The response of employment to the increase in demand would be magnified.

Given that the union places no value on an increase in employment, why is it possible for employment to rise with demand? This puzzle may appear particularly perplexing for the case where β rises with demand. In that case the union agrees to a decline in the bargained wage as demand rises; that is, members of the group of insiders who dominate union decision-making *lose* from a positive demand shift. The reason the union would be a party to such an agreement is that, in this model, the bargained wage is the result of a power-play between the union and the firm. The equilibrium wage balances the marginal gains of the two parties. For the firm, the marginal gain is influenced by changes in the wage. Higher wages reduce profits at a given level of employment. Because of this, firms wish to hold wages down. If they have some power, they can hold wages down, and as a result they will expand employment when demand increases.

The behaviour of the equilibrium wage implied by (8.4) is similar to the outcome of the group wage-setting models in chapters 6 and 7. Those models were not dominated by insiders: it appears that the nature of wage behaviour predicted by models of trades unions does not depend upon whether or not outsiders count.

8.2   The Range of Macroeconomic Equilibria

To derive the range of equilibria, we use the simple macroeconomic framework of the previous chapters. Assume an economy consisting of z producers who sell their output to retailers. Producers are identical, producing the same type of output by use of the same technology. The output is sold to retailers at the producer price, p^p. Competition forces p^p to equal the marginal cost of producing output. The many retailers are identical and sell in customer markets at a common retail price p. Consumers have to purchase output from retailers: they are unable to purchase directly from producers. The only variable cost for retailers is the purchase of goods from producers. Thus the marginal cost of supplying a good to a consumer is p^p.

Assuming that the elasticity of revenue with respect to employment, β, is constant, the bargained wage, determined by (8.4), is independent of the level of demand. The level of employment is determined by the equality of the money wage with the marginal revenue product of labour, equation (8.2). Deflating both sides of (8.2) by the retail price, p, gives the equation determining employment as

$$v = \frac{p^p}{p} f'(n) \qquad (8.5)$$

where $f(n)$ is the production function for producers. A particular value of the price ratio p^p/p determines the equilibrium level of employment. An increase in the price ratio p^p/p leads to no change in the bargained wage and an increase in the equilibrium level of employment. Because retailers sell in customer markets there is a range of equilibrium values of the ratio p^p/p and therefore a range of equilibrium levels of employment.

8.3 Aggregate Demand and Employment

As in the macroeconomic models of chapters 5, 6 and 7, the level of aggregate demand determines the equilibrium levels of employment at which the economy will settle. The analysis is so similar to that in chapter 7 (section 7.3) that there is no need to repeat it.

8.4 Calculating the Size of the Range of Equilibria

By assuming a constant value of the elasticity of revenue with respect to employment, the bargained wage is independent of the level of demand. Because of this, the range of equilibria can be calculated from (8.5). However, an explicit form for the production function has to be assumed. Take the constant elasticity form, $q = bn^\beta$. Then (8.5) becomes

$$v = \frac{p^p}{p} b\beta n^{\beta-1} \tag{8.6}$$

The minimum and maximum values of n are determined by the minimum and maximum values of the price ratio p^p/p. Thus n_{min} is determined by

$$v = \left(\frac{p^p}{p}\right)_{min} b\beta(n_{min})^{\beta-1} \tag{8.7}$$

and n_{max} is determined by

$$v = \left(\frac{p^p}{p}\right)_{max} b\beta(n_{max})^{\beta-1} \tag{8.8}$$

In both (8.7) and (8.8), v is determined by (8.4). Equating the right-hand sides of (8.7) and (8.8) and rearranging gives the equation determining the equilibrium range as

$$(n_{min}/n_{max}) = S^{1/(1-\beta)} \tag{8.9}$$

where $S = p^p_{min}/p^p_{max}$.

Equation (8.9) is the same as the equation determining the range in chapters 6 and 7. Therefore, in each model in which wages are determined by maximizing the welfare of a group, the size of the range is unaffected by the different assumptions made in these chapters.

8.5   Conclusion

The combination in a macroeconomic model of insider-dominated trades unions and customer market analysis has been shown in this chapter to yield a range of equilibrium levels of employment. The property of a range of macroeconomic equilibria is consistent with the pattern of inflation and unemployment observed in industrialized economies. On empirical grounds, equilibrium range models are superior to the other types of macroeconomic models in the current literature.

The process of wage determination modelled here uses a parameter representing the power of the trade union. This concept of union power is the ability to divide up, to the advantage of the union, the economic rents from employment. This power depends on the skill of the union wage negotiators and, perhaps, on the charisma of union leaders, that is their ability to hold members together and retain support during wage negotiations. The concept of power excludes some factors which, in general discussions, are sometimes thought of as aspects union power. Factors excluded from the concept of union power used in this chapter are the state of the labour market, the competitiveness of the firm in selling its output and the cost to the firm of a strike by the workers. These factors are captured by parameters in the model other than the power parameter. Thus the concept of power used in this chapter is more precise and narrow than the notion used in popular discussions. Indeed, the power parameter used here can, in principle, be measured by locating the bargained wage–employment outcome on the labour demand curve in relation to the zero-profit point and the point at which lay-off pay is equal to the marginal revenue product of labour.

Important topics for study are the factors which determine the value of the power parameter. While the value of the power parameter does not affect the size of the range of equilibrium, it does affect the bargained wage. Given the high cost of reducing inflation when there is a range of equilibria, the alternative of reducing union power suggests itself as a counter-inflationary policy. Reducing union power will have a once-and-for-all effect of lowering the bargained real wage, exerting a once-and-for-all negative impact on the price level. Furthermore, with a lower real wage, both the minimum and the maximum equilibrium levels of employment will be increased, improving the long-run choices of inflation and unemployment. The policy of corporatism attempts to induce unions to moderate their ambitions for wages, that is to voluntarily forego some of their power. In terms of the model of this chapter, this can be thought of as lowering the power parameter Φ.

Part 5
Macroeconomic Policy

9 The Implications for Macroeconomic Policy of a Range of Equilibrium Levels of Unemployment

The existence of a range of equilibrium rates of unemployment presents policy-makers with difficult choices. If the government pursues a non-discretionary policy of aggregate demand management such as a monetary rule specifying a constant growth rate of a monetary aggregate, then only by a fluke will unemployment settle at the minimum equilibrium rate (which will be called MINEQUN). On the other hand, an activist policy of aggregate demand management that aims at keeping the rate of unemployment at the MINEQUN level runs the risk of generating inflation.

9.1 Gradual Inflation

Consider figure 9.1, which shows MINEQUN and the maximum equilibrium level of unemployment, MAXEQUN. Assume for now that the MINEQUN is known and that the government has been able to set aggregate demand at a level such that the rate of unemployment is equal to MINEQUN. Further more, assume that the rate of inflation is initially at zero. The economy is at point A in figure 9.1.

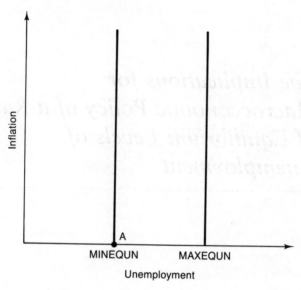

Figure 9.1

Starting at A, a positive shock to aggregate demand, such as a temporary increase in the demand for exports by overseas residents, will push unemployment below MINEQUN, create excess demand in the product and labour markets and cause an increase in the price level and the wage level. Assuming that this shock disappears before people's expectations about inflation are affected, then the economy will return to A with a higher price level and a higher wage level. For the economy not to overshoot A to a rate of unemployment greater than MINEQUN requires an aggregate demand policy to accommodate the increase in the price level by, for example, an increase in the money supply.

Now, again starting at A, consider a negative shock to aggregate demand. A temporary decrease in the level of aggregate demand will push the rate of unemployment above MINEQUN. For a shock which is not large enough to push unemployment above MAXEQUN, the price level and wage level will not fall. When the shock disappears and aggregate demand returns to its former level, the rate of unemployment will return to MINEQUN. However, the price level and wage level will not have changed from their former levels. The negative shock to aggregate demand will have left the price level unaffected.

From this analysis of a positive demand shock and a negative demand shock, it follows that a random sequence of shocks which causes unemployment to fluctuate around MINEQUN will cause the price level to increase. A policy which aims for MINEQUN and which cannot neutralize positive demand shocks will be associated with a positive rate of inflation.

A negative shock to aggregate demand that pushes the rate of unemployment above the MAXEQUN level will exert some downward pressure on the price level and wage level. However, it is reasonable to ignore such a shock in the context of an aggregate demand policy aimed at keeping the average rate of unemployment at the MINEQUN level. From the models in the earlier chapters the size of the range of equilibrium rates of unemployment is several percentage points, and a range of that magnitude will dominate most of the shocks to the level of aggregate demand that an economy is likely to experience.

9.2 Increasing Inflation

A policy which aims to have the average rate of unemployment equal to MINEQUN may generate increasing inflation. In the analysis of the previous section it was shown that with a zero expected rate of inflation, a sequence of random shocks to the level of aggregate demand yielded a rate of inflation that averaged a positive value. It is reasonable to argue that this creeping inflation will eventually cause people to revise upwards their view of the expected rate of inflation. After an upward revision is made to the expected rate of inflation, positive shocks to the level of aggregate demand will lead to larger increases in the price and wage levels than they would if the expected rate of inflation were zero. Furthermore, negative shocks will be associated with positive inflation rather than with zero inflation.

To avoid the increase of inflation, aggregate demand policy would have to aim for an average rate of unemployment that is greater than the MINEQUN rate. Just how much greater depends on two factors. These are the size of the range of equilibrium rates of unemployment (that is, the difference between MINEQUN and MAXEQUN) and the size of the shocks to the rate of unemployment. The relative size of these two factors determines the target rate of unemployment. There are two cases:

(1) The first case is one in which the largest possible shock to aggregate demand changes the rate of unemployment by *less* than half the size of the range of equilibrium rates of unemployment. In this case a target rate of unemployment which exceeds MINEQUN by the amount of the largest possible shock will prevent unemployment ever being pushed below MINEQUN and so will insulate the economy against inflation. Of course, the impact on unemployment of shocks to the level of aggregate demand is not outside the control of policy-makers. For example, automatic stabilizers can dampen the impact of shocks to aggregate demand and so allow policy-makers to aim at a lower target rate of unemployment without risking inflation.

(2) The second case is one in which the largest possible shock to aggregate demand changes the rate of unemployment by *more* than half the size of the range of equilibrium rates of unemployment. In this case a target rate of unemployment halfway between MINEQUN and MAXEQUN can be aimed at. In deducing the target as this level, the shocks are assumed to be symmetrically distributed. With a symmetrical distribution periods of rising prices, which occur when unemployment is below MINEQUN, will be offset by periods of falling prices, which occur when unemployment is above MAXEQUN. On average the price level will show no tendency to rise or fall.

9.3   The Problem of Locating MINEQUN

The discussion so far has not faced up to a major practical problem. In practice, the rates of MINEQUN and MAXEQUN are not known with much precision. Our ignorance of these rates increases the risk that aggregate demand policy will induce an increasing rate of inflation. If the estimate by policy-makers of MINEQUN is below the true rate, then an unreasonably low target rate of unemployment may be selected. By selecting such a low target, unemployment will on occasion be below MINEQUN, and this will cause inflation to increase.

In addition to the usual econometric problems of estimation, such as problems of inaccurate data and incorrect model specification, the estimation of MINEQUN and MAXEQUN is hampered by their being at the edges of a range of equilibria. Compare the estimation of the edges of a range of equilibrium rates of unemployment with the estimation of the natural rate of unemployment. For a hypothetical economy with a natural rate of unemployment, rates of unemployment each side of the natural rate yield opposite impacts on the levels of prices and wages. Unemployment below the natural rate will exert upward pressure on prices and wages, while unemployment in excess of the natural rate will exert downward pressure on prices and wages. For an economy with a range of equilibrium rates of unemployment, the contrast between the impact on prices and wages of unemployment in excess of MINEQUN, and unemployment of less than MINEQUN is not so marked. Instead of observing 'up' or 'down' as unemployment varies, the pattern observed would be 'up' or 'no change' as unemployment fluctuates around MINEQUN.

In models of the natural rate of unemployment, variables which influence the natural rate have been identified. Friedman (1968) asserted that minimum wage laws and the strength of trades unions would increase the natural rate. However, as the survey by Johnson and Layard (1986) makes clear, attempts to measure the impact on the natural rate of these and other variables, such as unemployment benefits, have not been very successful. In models with a range of equilibrium rates of unemployment, it is the MINEQUN level which will be influenced by these variables. By influencing the boundary of a range, the impact of these variables will be harder to measure. Consider, for example, the pattern of unemployment benefits in Australia in the 1970s. In 1973 there was a substantial rise in unemployment benefits as a ratio of average weekly earnings. At that time the inflation–unemployment trade-off worsened significantly, indicating, to those who use the natural rate model, an increase in the natural rate of unemployment. Subsequently, the unemployment benefit ratio declined but the inflation–unemployment trade-off did not improve. Viewed from the perspective of the models of a natural rate of unemployment this pattern is puzzling. Viewed from the perspective of the models of a range of equilibrium rates of unemployment this pattern can be explained. The rise in the unemployment benefit ratio raised MINEQUN. The subsequent fall lowered MINEQUN but left the economy within the range of equilibria, causing no deflationary impact.

There is a very serious implication of the existence of a range of equilibrium rates of unemployment. If the tools of aggregate demand management have to be relied on then it is extremely expensive to discover the MINEQUN rate without causing inflation. To discover the MINEQUN rate requires pushing the actual rate of unemployment below MINEQUN. This follows because, without a rise in the price level, one cannot know where MINEQUN is. However, then to reduce the price level using aggregate demand policy requires a rate of unemployment in excess of MAXEQUN. By constrast, in an economy with a natural rate of unemployment the discovery of the natural rate is far less costly. A rise in the price level caused by unemployment below the natural rate can be offset by unemployment above the natural rate. With an equilibrium range there is the added burden of pushing unemployment through the range.

Consider the expected cost of lowering unemployment using aggregate demand in a situation where the long-run aim is for the rate of inflation not to increase. To calculate this expected cost, the probability that unemployment will be pushed below MINEQUN has to be multiplied by the output loss of a period of unemployment in excess of MAXEQUN. If the equilibrium range is two percentage points of unemployment then this is a large cost. If the range is 10, 20 or 30 percentage points the cost is staggering. Furthermore, it is unlikely that MINEQUN is constant in any economy. MINEQUN cannot be assumed to remain fixed once it has been discovered. To attempt to discover MINEQUN by lowering unemployment, that is to determine how far one can go raising aggregate demand, is to risk a large cost in return for knowledge which may be useful for only a limited period of time.

9.4 Reducing Inflation

In the previous section it was argued that the existence of a range of equilibrium rates of unemployment can make aggregate demand management an expensive policy to use to reduce the rate of inflation. The aggregate demand policy would require that unemployment be raised above MAXEQUN in order to reduce inflation. The larger the size of the range and the higher the rate of MAXEQUN the more expensive is a policy of deflation for reducing inflation. Leaving aside aggregate demand management, there are two other policies which can be used to reduce the rate of inflation. These are a prices and incomes policy and a policy of tax cuts.

9.4.1 Prices and incomes policies

By inducing firms and workers to set prices and wages below the levels which they consider to be optimal, a prices and incomes policy can reduce the rate of inflation. Firms may be induced to sacrifice some or all of a possible price increase opened up by the upward movement of the demand curve they face. According to efficiency-wage theory, if firms do not increase wages by the optimal amount, they may lose some efficiency or may have to increase expenditures on monitoring employees. However, by appeals to the national interest, workers may be induced to forgo a wage rise without curtailing their efforts. Turning to the cases where wages are set to maximize the welfare of a group of workers, the cases of a labour pool sharing the rents from specific human capital and of a trade union extracting rents from those who purchase labour, a prices and incomes policy may persuade the group to forgo some group welfare.

In the instances cited above, prices and incomes policies reduce inflation by inducing some people or groups to make sacrifices. They are induced to forgo the achievement of their objectives. Provided that the economy was within the equilibrium range, it may be that a fairly sharp reduction in inflation could follow from such restraint. Outside the equilibrium range, incomes policies at rates of unemployment below MINEQUN are an attempt to keep the lid on disequilibrium forces. These forces would be pushing up inflation. Within the equilibrium range, once the expected rate of inflation is reduced the actual rate of inflation would fall. Furthermore, the sacrifices called upon are temporary. Once inflation has fallen to tolerable levels, restraint is no longer needed.

In an industralized economy the wages of different groups of workers are set at different times. Prices of products are also set at different times. Because of the staggered nature of wage- and price-setting, prices and incomes policies can require some groups to make disproportionate sacrifices. Groups for whom a price or wage rise was due at the time a prices and incomes policy was introduced will suffer compared with groups who have just enjoyed a price or wage rise. Such inequities can place severe strains on a prices and incomes policy, especially if reliance is placed on voluntary compliance.

9.4.2 Tax cuts and monetary tightness

The price level may be reduced by tax cuts which decrease the marginal cost of output sufficiently to induce firms to cut prices. Increases in interest rates also may reduce the price level by decreasing the prices of real assets. Policies of cutting taxes and of tightening monetary policy have been discussed by Perkins (1979). If unemployment is within the equilibrium range then varying the policy mix towards fiscal ease and monetary restraint can reduce inflation. However, a change towards fiscal ease and monetary tightness may reduce investment spending and lead to a deterioration in the trade balance. These consequences would reduce the consumption possibilities of society in the future. Therefore, using tax cuts and monetary tightness to reduce inflation may impose a cost of a lower level of consumption for people in the future. In McDonald (1984a) it is shown that the lower the rate of tax the greater is the likelihood that the level of consumption in the future will suffer from a policy of cutting taxes and raising interest rates. Thus the policy of cutting taxes has an inherent limit. Reducing taxes will eventually crowd out investment and/or the production of traded goods. Future levels of consumption would then suffer.

9.5 Reducing the Size of the Range of Equilibrium Levels of Unemployment

The cost of reducing inflation by a restrictive aggregate demand policy can be decreased if the MAXEQUN rate itself can be lowered. In order to reduce inflation by restricting aggregate demand, unemployment has to be pushed above the MAXEQUN rate. With a lower MAXEQUN, unemployment has to be pushed up by less and the loss of output entailed in bringing into operation the disequilibrium forces of excess supply is less.

Since the equilibrium range has been derived from customer market analysis it is natural to look there for insights about ways to control inflation. Recall that in customer markets, consumers are slow to find out about any relative price changes posted by shops which they *do not* patronize. This slow acquisition of knowledge reduces the incentive for shops to price-compete. Firms will cut price only if marginal costs are reduced relative to price by the crucial margin. The crucial margin is the size of the step in the firm's marginal revenue curve. One proposal which may increase the speed of information flow is that shops be required by law to display their own price index (see McDonald, 1984b, 1987). In construction of the index, the price that the shop charges for each of its goods would be weighted by the share of sales of that good in the shop's total sales. This index would be updated regularly (say, weekly) and be displayed outside the shop and in all advertisements by that shop. All shops would use a common date for the base of their indexes. A common base would help consumers to make price level comparisons between competing stores. The idea is that these indexes would increase the flow of information about price changes to potential customers. An advantage of an index is that it is a single summary statistic that could provide a cheap, easily advertised source of information which the potential customer could use when comparing suppliers. An alternative, under which shops provide lists of the prices of products they sell, seems a more difficult basis for making comparisons.

By advertising its price index, a retailer confers an external benefit on the economy. Consumers can use this information to aid their evaluation of the prices charged by other firms. Thus the social benefits of a price index exceed the private benefits to the retailer. Because of this divergence of social benefits from private benefits, the privately optimal actions of retailers will not lead to a socially optimal outcome. There is a case for forcing shops to advertise their price indexes.

Of course, the proposed index is only a summary statistic and so is a rather rough guide to the price of the good or the bundle of goods which is of interest to a particular customer. For this reason the display of the index may not be sufficient to give consumers enough information to eliminate the step in the marginal revenue curve. However, there is some empirical evidence which is encouraging. Devine and Marion (1979) report that following the publication of price information for several supermarkets in Ottawa–Hull, Canada, food prices declined by 7.1 per cent over a 6-week period compared with a decline of 0.6 per cent in the control market. The price information disseminated included a store price index as well as a number of prices for individual food items. These results suggest a sizeable response of prices to published information on prices.

By reducing the size of the step in the marginal revenue curve facing retailers, the price index proposal would reduce the size of the range of equilibrium rates of unemployment and would draw MAXEQUN closer to MINEQUN. Given that the increase in competitiveness in the retail market would not be expected to increase MINEQUN, the introduction of these price indexes would reduce the cost of a restrictive aggregate demand policy aimed at reducing inflation.

Part 6
Conclusion

10 Conclusion

In this book the theory of the range of equilibrium rates of unemployment has been developed. Ranges of equilibrium rates of unemployment have been derived from four macroeconomic models. At any rate of unemployment within the range of equilibria, the rate of inflation tends to be constant. Instead of the vertical long-run Phillips curve of the natural rate model, in the models of this book there is a range of unemployment rates separating the zone of increasing inflation from the zone of decreasing inflation.

Within the range of equilibrium, the real level of aggregate demand determines the actual level of unemployment at which the economy settles. Because of this property, the models offer a microfoundation for Keynesian economics.

The analysis of the setting of retail prices in a customer market is the common feature of each of the four models. Customer market analysis is the crucial ingredient from which a range of equilbria may be reasonably derived.

In the models the ranges are ranges of involuntary unemployment. The unemployed would prefer to be employed but wages do not adjust to open up the required level of job vacancies. This involuntary unemployment was due to efficiency-wage theory in the first model and, in the other three models, due to groups of workers seeking to maximize their collective welfare. These groups of workers were throught of as either loosely organized groups seeking to share the rents accruing from specific human capital, or as organized by trades unions.

For each model, calculations of the size of the range of equilibrium rates of unemployment were made. These calculations suggest that the models based on groups maximizing their collective interest yield larger ranges of equilibria than does the model based on efficiency-wage theory. The models are simple and so these calculations should be treated as a very rough guide to reality. However, the ordering of the models of the maximization of group welfare relative to the efficiency-wage model may survive on extending the models to more sophisticated versions.

The models should be seen as complements rather than substitutes. In an industrialized economy one would expect different sectors to have different mechanisms of wage determination. In some sectors aggressive unions may dominate. In others efficiency-wage theory may dominate. A grand macroeconomic model would combine these mechanisms of wage determination, and, perhaps, add a sector operating on conventional competitive lines. Such a macroeconomic model has not been attempted here.

If the mechanisms of wage determination analysed in this book are accepted as a classification of labour market structures, then the natural question that arises is how to explain them. Why might one industry be characterized by a particular mechanism of wage determination? The mechanisms based on maximizing group welfare have been presented in an order which suggests an historical development. Specific human capital generates rents. Workers form into groups to protect their share of these rents. The functioning of these groups is aided by adopting a more formal trade union structure. But the subsequent increase in power leads to efforts by the unionized group to appropriate other rents from the employer, such as the rents from monopoly power in selling the product.

The implications of the models for government policy towards inflation and unemployment were discussed in chapter 9. The models imply the rather dismal conclusion that by aiming for a low rate of unemployment at or near the minimum equilibrium level, the rate of inflation will tend to increase. Furthermore, to try to reduce inflation by the traditional tools of aggregate demand is an expensive option in the equilibrium range model. In consequence, to discover the size of the minimum equilibrium rate of unemployment, policy-makers face the choice of either allowing inflation to increase or suffering periods of very high unemployment. This dilemma would not be so difficult if the size of the equilibrium range of unemployment could be reduced. From the analysis of customer markets one proposal to reduce the size of the range of equilibria was deduced: this is a proposal for shops to display indexes of their prices. However, it has to be added that it is not clear how effective this proposal would be in practice. Because of the costs suffered by people as a result of unemployment and inflation, experimentation on the lines of the price index proposal would be worthwhile.

References

Becker, G. S. 1962: Investment in human capital: a theoretical analysis. *Journal of Political Economy*, 70 (Supplement) 9–49.

Blanchard, O. J. and Summers, L. H. 1986: Hysteresis and the European unemployment problem. In S. Fischer (ed.), *NBER Macroeconomics Annual*, Cambridge, Mass.: MIT Press, 15–77.

Borland, J. I. 1985: The economic analysis of trade unions. M.A. thesis, University of Melbourne.

Brown, C. and Medoff, J. 1978: Trade unions in the production process, *Journal of Political Economy*, 86, 355–78.

Brown, J. N. and Ashenfelter, O. 1986: Testing the efficiency of employment contracts. *Journal of Political Economy*, 94(3, part 2), S40–87.

Carruth, A. A. and Oswald, A. J. 1987: On union preferences and labour market models: insiders and outsiders. *Economic Journal*, 97, 431–45.

Chapman, P. G. and Fisher, M. R. 1984: Union wage policies: comment. *American Economic Review*, 74 September, 755–8.

de Menil, G. 1971: *Bargaining: Monopoly Power Versus Union Power*. Cambridge, Mass.: MIT Press.

Devine, D. G. and Marion, B. W. 1979: The influence of consumer price information on retail pricing and consumer behaviour. *American Journal of Agricultural Economics*, 61(2), 228–37.

Diamond, P. A. 1981: Mobility costs, frictional unemployment and efficiency. *Journal of Political Economy*, 89(4), 798–812.

Diamond, P. A. 1982: Aggregate demand management in search equilibrium. *Journal of Political Economy*, 90(5), 881–94.

Dickens, W. and Katz, L. 1986: Inter-industry wage differences and industry characteristics. In K. Lang and J. Leonard (eds), *Unemployment and the Structure of Labour Markets*. Oxford: Basil Blackwell, 48–89.

Douglas, E. 1962: Size of firm and the structure of costs in retailing. *Journal of Business*, 35, 158–90.

138 References

Eberts, R. W. and Stone, J. A. 1986: On the contract curve: a test of alternative models of collective bargaining. *Journal of Labour Economics*, 4(1), 66–81.

Friedman, M. 1968: The role of monetary policy. *American Economic Review*, 58(1), 1–17.

Griffith, G. R. 1974: Sydney meat marketing margins – an econometric analysis. *Review of Marketing and Agricultural Economics*, 42(4), 223–38.

Hall, R. E. 1980: Employment fluctuations and wage rigidity. *Brookings Papers on Economic Activity*, 1980, 91–141.

Hargreaves-Heap, S. P. 1980: Choosing the wrong 'natural' rate: accelerating inflation or decelerating employment and growth? *Economic Journal* 90(359), 611–20.

Hashimoto, M. and Yu, B. T. 1980: Specific capital, employment contracts and wage rigidity. *Bell Journal of Economics*, 11(2), 536–49.

Howitt, P. 1985: Transactions costs in the theory of unemployment. *American Economic Review*, 75(1), 88–100.

Jackson, D. 1982: *Introduction to Economics*. London: Macmillan.

Johnson, G. E. and Layard, P. R. G. 1986: The natural rate of unemployment: explanation and policy. In O.C. Ashenfelter and R. Layard (eds), *Handbook of Labor Economics*, vol II. Amsterdam: North-Holland, 921–99.

Kohls, R. L. and Uhl, J. N. 1980: *Marketing of Agricultural Products*, 5th edn. New York: Macmillan.

Krueger, A. B. and Summers, L. H. 1988: Efficiency wages and the inter-industry wage structure. *Econometrica*, 56, 259–93.

Lindbeck, A. and Snower, D.J. 1984: Involuntary unemployment as an insider–outsider dilemma. Seminar paper no. 282, *Institute for International Economic Studies*, University of Stockholm.

Lindbeck, A. and Snower, D. J. 1985: Explanations of unemployment. *Oxford Review of Economic Policy*, 1(2), 34–59.

Lindbeck, A. and Snower, D. J. 1988a: Cooperation, harassment, and involuntary unemployment: an insider–outsider approach. *American Economic Review*, 78(1), 167–88.

Lindbeck, A. and Snower, D. J. 1988b: Long-term unemployment and macro-economic policy. *American Economic Review*, 78(2), 38–43.

MacCurdy, T. E. and Pencavel, J. H. 1986: Testing competing models of wage and employment determination in unionised markets. *Journal of Political Economy*, 94(3, part 2), S3–39.

Marceau, I. W. 1967: Quarterly estimates of the demand and price structure for meat in New South Wales. *Australian Journal of Agricultural Economics*, 11 (June), 49–62.

McDonald, I. M. 1984a: Anti-stagflationary tax cuts and the problem of investment. *Economic Record*, 60(170), 284–93.

McDonald, I. M. 1984b: Trying to understand stagflation. *Australian Economic Review*, 3'84, 32–56.

McDonald, I. M. 1987: Customer markets, trade unions and stagflation. *Economica*, 54, 139–53.

McDonald, I. M. 1989a: Insiders and trade union power. Mimeo, University of Melbourne.

McDonald, I. M. 1989b: The wage demands of a plant specific trade union. *Oxford Economic Papers*, 41, 506–27.

McDonald, I. M. and Solow, R. M. 1980: Trade unions, wages and employment. Paper presented at the Ninth Conference of Economists, Brisbane.

McDonald, I. M. and Solow, R. M. 1981: Wage bargaining and employment. *American Economic Review*, 71, 896–908.

McDonald, I. M. and Solow, R. M. 1984: Union wage policies: reply. *American Economic Review*, 74(4), 759–61.

McDonald, I. M. and Spindler, K. J. 1987: An empirical investigation of customer market analysis – a microfoundation for macroeconomics. *Applied Economics*, 19, 1149–74.

Mitchell, W. F. 1987: The nairu, structural imbalance and the macroequilibrium unemployment rate. *Australian Economic Papers* 26(48), 101–18.

Mortensen, D. T. 1970: Job search, the duration of unemployment and the Phillips curve. *American Economic Review*, 60(5), 847–62.

Naughtin J. C. 1977: Retail marketing margins in Victoria: a trading accounts approach. Unpubl. M. Agric. Sci. thesis, La Trobe University, Melbourne.

Naughtin, J. C. and Quilkey, J. J. 1979: Pricing efficiency in the retail meat market. *Australian Journal of Agricultural Economics*, 23(1), 48–61.

Nickell, S. J. 1986: Dynamic models of labour demand. In O. C. Ashenfelter and R. Layard (eds), *Handbook of Labour Economics*, vol. 1. Amsterdam: North Holland, 473–522.

Oswald, A. J. 1985: The economic theory of trade unions: an introductory survey. *The Scandinavian Journal of Economics*, 87(2), 160–93.

Oswald, A. J. unpublished: Efficient contracts are on the labour demand curve: theory and facts. Centre of Labour Economics, London School of Economics.

Parish, R. M. 1966: Price levelling and averaging. *Farm Economist*, 11(5), 187–98.

Perkins, J. O. N. 1979: *The macroeconomic mix to stop inflation*. London: Macmillan.

Phelps, E. S. 1970: Money wage dynamics and labor market equilibrium. In E. S. Phelps (ed.), *Microeconomic Foundations of Employment and Inflation Theory*. New York: Norton, 124–68.

Phelps, E. S. and Winters, S. J. 1970: Optimal price policy under atomistic competition. In E. S. Phelps (ed.), *Microeconomic Foundations of Employment and Inflation Theory*. New York: Norton, 309–37.

Phillips, A. W. 1958: The relation between unemployment and the rate of change of money wages rates in the United Kingdom, 1861–1957. *Economica*, 25, 483–99.

Prices Justification Tribunal 1978: *Beef Marketing and Processing*. Melbourne.

Rotemberg, J. J. and Saloner, G. 1986: A supergame-theoretic model of price wars during booms. *American Economic Review*, 76, 390–407.

Shapiro, C. and Stiglitz, J. E. 1984 Equilibrium unemployment as a worker discipline device. *American Economic Review*, 74, 433–44.

Sibly, H. 1988: Modelling information flows in customer markets. Mimeo, University of Melbourne.

Sibly, H. 1989: The timing of search in customer markets. Mimeo, University of Melbourne.

Solow, R. M. 1979: Another possible source of wage stickiness. *Journal of Macroeconomics*, 1, 79–82.

Solow, R. M. 1985: Insiders and outsiders in wage determination. *Scandinavian Journal of Economics*, 87, 411–28.

Stiglitz, J. E. 1987: Competition and the number of firms in a market: are duopolies more competitive than atomistic markets? *Journal of Political Economy*, 95, 1041–61.

Tobin, J. 1972: Inflation and unemployment. *American Economic Review*, 62, 1–18.

Tucker, K. A. 1975: *Economies of Scale in Retailing*. Farnborough, England: Saxon House.

Watson, A. S. and Parish, R. M. 1982: Marketing agricultural products. In D. B. Williams (ed.), *Agriculture in the Australian Economy*, 2nd edn. Sydney: Sydney University Press.

Williams, W. F. and Stout, T. T. 1964: *Economics of the Livestock–Meat Industry*, New York: Macmillan.

Woglom, G. 1982: Underemployment equilibrium with rational expectations. *Quarterly Journal of Economics*, 97, 89–107.

Yellen, J. L. 1984: Efficiency wage models of unemployment. *American Economic Review*, 74 (Papers and Proceedings), 200–5.

Index